ALBANIA TRAVEL GUIDE 2020

EMSAL AJREDINI

OPPIAN

Published by Oppian Press
Helsinki, Finland

ISBN 978-951-877-171-8

GETTING TO KNOW ALBANIA

Are you planning to visit Albania? If yes, then read on to find out about this small and warm country, the so-called *"Land of the Eagles"* due to its historical ties to the symbol of the two-headed eagle. In Albanian literature and folklore, the eagle appears as a symbol of heroism and freedom, and Albanians often refer to themselves as the *"Sons of the Eagle."*

This unique Mediterranean destination is a thrilling and charming exotic locale, yet, vastly unexplored in depth. Only in the recent years it has become a popular destination for visitors around the world. So, you will be able to explore this country's wonders without having to come across some excessive commercials. With pristine beaches and lofty peaks, along with untouched lakes, historical Roman ruins, vibrant Ottoman towns and its rich culture; Albania has variety of things to offer you to have the adventure of a lifetime.

However, planning a trip can be tiring and overwhelming, especially if you don't know what you need to consider when doing it. Hopefully, this travel guide book will help you to save some money, time and your sanity. Read on to find out how to experience Europe like you have never seen before in this small land!

Geographical position

Albania is a beautiful and small coastal country found in the Southwestern Europe, the Western part of the Balkan Peninsula. It is positioned on the Adriatic and Ionian Sea inside the Mediterranean Sea, with a beautiful coastline of about 476 km (296 mi).

Borderline

The complete borderline of Albania is 1,094 km, which is consisted of 657 km land boundary, 316 km maritime boundary, 48 km river boundary and 73 km lake boundary.

Albania is bounded by Montenegro to the northwest, by Kosovo to the northeast, by the Republic of Macedonia to the east and Greece to the southeast and south. Italy lies across the Mediterranean to the west; at its narrowest point, close to where the Adriatic and the Ionian Seas meet, Albania and Italy are only 75 km (47 miles) apart.

While your visit to Albania you can use the opportunity to visit and explore one or more other Balkan countries. They are close to one another and easily accessible too.

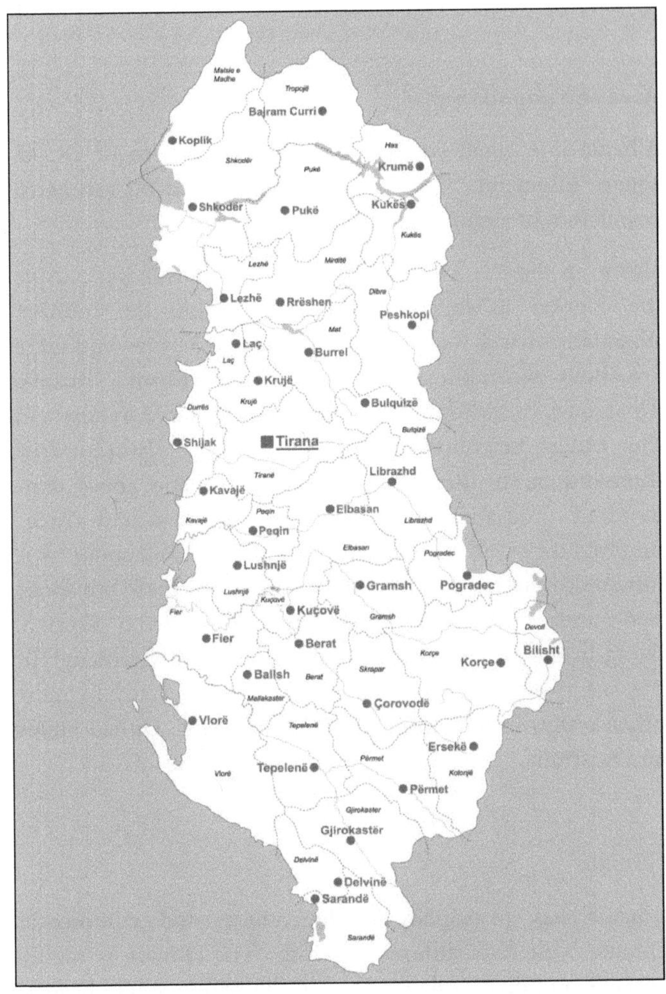
Bajram Curri
Koplik
Krumë
Shkodër
Pukë
Kukës
Lezhë
Rrëshen
Peshkopi
Laç
Burrel
Krujë
Bulqizë
Shijak
Tirana
Librazhd
Kavajë
Elbasan
Peqin
Lushnjë
Gramsh
Pogradec
Kuçovë
Fier
Berat
Bilisht
Korçe
Ballsh
Çorovodë
Vlorë
Ersekë
Tepelenë
Përmet
Gjirokastër
Delvinë
Sarandë

Area and population

Albania is a small country with a defined area of 28,748 square kilometers (11,100 square miles) and an estimated population of about 3,029,278 (2015 EST.)

However, there is a vast number of Albanians living outside the country as much as they live within the country. Albanians own two countries, Albania and Kosovo and there are about two million Albanians living in Kosovo (Kosovo Albanians). In addition, there are large registered numbers in the other neighboring countries; about five-hundred thousand in the Republic of Macedonia, and about one-hundred thousand in Montenegro, an estimated three-hundred thousand immigrants live in Greece and about two-hundred thousand reside in Italy. Moreover, there are about two-hundred thousand Albanians, mostly from Kosovo, living in the central Europe (Switzerland and Germany). In the last twenty years, Albanians have immigrated to most other countries of Europe, as well as Canada, United States and Australia.

Climate

Albania has principally Mediterranean and continental climate with four different seasons. The climate is highly variable and diverse depending on the region you're headed to. It usually has hot, dry summers and cool, wet winters in the lowlands. The temperature ranges between –1 °C in winter and can go up to 40 °C during summer.

The warmest areas of the country are closely located along the coasts of the Ionian and Adriatic Seas, while the coldest areas are located in the eastern and northern highlands. In these areas, snowfall commonly occurs from November until March, particularly on the mountains in the north and east, including the Albanian Alps and Korab Mountains. The towns around these mountains are usually very cold throughout this period of the year.

Clothes you will need to bring depend on the time of the year, the places and regions you will be visiting, and the activities you have planned. For outdoor activities in the mountains warm and waterproof clothing will be necessary every time of the year. During the summer nights along the coast, long trousers and a light jacket will often be required.

In order to find out what is the best time to visit Albania and plan your perfect vacation, read on the following section!

Seasonality

The best time to visit Albania is during the shoulder seasons, which take part between mid-March - June, and September - October. During these times of the year, the weather is just right - it is not too hot, and it is not too cold, making it ideal for those who want to enjoy a mountain or a beach holiday and explore the great outdoors.

During spring time, between the mid-March and June, the weather in Albania is really enjoyable in the coastal areas and in the mountains as well, especially in the western part of the country. This is the finest time to visit Albania for relaxing by the coast, as the winter cold is left behind, and the hot summer days have not started yet. If you happen to visit Albania during spring time, you can explore and enjoy the striking locales and the beaches of the Ionian Coast and the Albanian Riviera. Especially, the beginning of the spring is one of the best times of the year to visit Albania if you are fan of traditional festivals and events. Numerous events and concerts are frequently held by the Riviera which can spice up your holiday during this period too. One of the most important pagan festivals called *Dita e Veres* (the Summer Day, although its spring yet) is celebrated in the country on 14th March. If you visit Albania during this time make sure to celebrate this festival in Elbasan, a town located just one hour driving from Tirana. During this day, people of all ages celebrate the first day of spring by dancing, singing, drinking, taking part in parades. On that day also try the special cookie called *ballokume* (tasty cookie made with corn flour, butter, sugar and egg yolks).

July to August is the highest season for tourism in Albania, and the main tourist stream are Albanians who live abroad and come back to their homeland to spend their holidays. however, there will still be far fewer tourists in Albania than there will be in the rest of the other European countries, so you won't have heavy crowds to worry about.

The heat in the coastal areas will be scorching which will prevent you from exploring the country in relaxation. However, if you want to escape the summer heat you can head to explore the mountain areas. The summer is very enjoyable in the mountains, especially the peaks of Thethi and Boga, high up in the Albanian Alps. You can go hiking and explore the beauty of the mountains and the Grunas Waterfall.

September and October are the other two of the best months to visit Albania. Fall is just beautiful in Albania, its colors show up everywhere and summer heat is already gone. The weather is quite pleasant, even though the evenings might be a little cool. This period of the year is a superb time to go exploring the outdoors. However, the weather in the mountains will get really cold, while the coastal areas will be chilly and you won't be able to go swimming either. This is a shoulder season in Albania, and if you don't mind the weather you can visit during this period and enjoy your trip without having to worry about the crowds. During this season you might want to stick to urban areas and visit some of the most attractive towns. You can head over to Gjirokastra, a UNESCO site and an old and well-preserved Ottoman town with its charming houses and castles. Furthermore, you can also visit Berat, also called the city of 1001 windows, it is a fortified city filled with houses, churches and mosques. Kruja, known for its stunning architecture, is another place you should definitely visit.

November to beginning of March is the winter period, and is the low season in Albania. Visiting Albania during this period is not much recommended as the winters are usually cold. So, you will not be able to spend time along the coast or do outdoor activities such as hiking in the mountains. However, if you want a budget trip this a good period to visit cities and small Albanian towns especially during the time of the Albanian Independence Day as well as the Christmas time. They are definitely sights to behold! The capital city, Tirana is the place where the most important New Year's celebrations take place. So, keep in mind that if you want a unique way to spend the New Year's Eve, go straight to the city square and celebrate it among thousands Albanians, while enjoying the fireworks, music and concerts.

During the winter season, if you don't want to spend your holiday in urban areas and instead you want to enjoy gorgeous winter scenery, go to Korca, a city located near the Macedonian and Greek border and one of the most important and charming ski destinations in Albania. The locals usually spend their winter holidays in this beautiful region where there are plenty of opportunities for outdoor activities such as skiing, ice skating and hiking. Korca is a historical city with a lovely café culture. So after a cold day in the nearby mountains, go for a visit to the city center, relax, get a hot drink and warm up in of the cafés at *Pazari i Vjeter.*

CULTURE, TRADITION AND LAWS

ALBANIA HAS HAD A HISTORY OF COMMUNISM AND VIOLENCE which drove away the tourists and unfortunately, the aftermath stuck in minds of many people. However, today's modern Albania is welcoming and eager to show its true wonders, all you have to do is talk to somebody who recently has visited Albania.

One of the most beautiful things about Albania is that it is a religiously tolerant country. Christians, Muslims, Jews and members of other belief systems feel safe and welcomed in this country. Take a walk in any town and within few meters distance you will come across Orthodox churches, Catholic churches and mosques.

Albanians are remarkably hospitable, generous and warm nation. Albanian families spend a lot of money on visitor's meals and a guest invited for dinner or lunch will be given huge amounts of food. If you are invited and are visiting an Albanian house, be prepared to be served copious amounts of meat and Albanian *raki* (a strong and intense aromatic liqueur very similar to grappa as it is made from grape pomace). It is a form of courtesy that when you visit an Albanian family, you bring a small and symbolic present for the host, as a sign of your gratitude. It is in Albanian culture that when greeting each other they shake hands and in many cases, they kiss each other on the cheeks, usually three to four times.

Albanians will do anything to make you comfortable at their homes. *'Buke e kripe, e zemer'* is an old Albanian saying which means: *'Bread and salt, and heart.'* This saying depicts exactly how they would welcome a guest visiting their home; they will serve you whatever they have at home, even if it means just bread and salt, but sure will do anything to make you feel welcomed.

Furthermore, it is an old and strong tradition that if you were a traveller and you seek a place to sleep, you could simply knock on the first house you found and asked the owner if he or she wanted a guest, and the owner would without more ado find a spare bed or room for you to rest and sleep. So, if someone comes at your house looking for help, you give them a place to stay. This tradition has been passed down for centuries as part of *the Kanun of Lekë Dukagjini,* which is like a code or a set of customary laws created in the 15th Century. This code stated that *'Before the house belongs to the owner, it first belongs to God and the guest.'*

One of the strongest principles of Albanian people is *"besa"* which means that if you give your word for something, you got to keep it. It is due to their given word that no single Jew was given to Nazis by Albania. Albania was among few countries that protected the Jews during World War II. Albanians are known for being brave and trustworthy nation with some really strong traditions. However, throughout the time many traditions have faded away, yet, their generous hospitality, their welcoming nature and reliability have remained loyal.

Albanian national and ethnic symbol is the eagle with two heads, which is used in the national flag of the country, in postcards, traditional costumes and handicrafts, literature and history.

The official language is Albanian. It is a specific language that does not resemble any other language in Europe. Albanian language is ancient and has its own branch in the linguistic tree. Albanians are really proud of their language, so they will really like it and it will be really nice of you if you learn few basic words and phrases. For instance: Mirëmëngjes (Good morning), Mirëdita (Good afternoon), Mirëmbrëma (Good evening), Mirupafshim (Goodbye, see you), Natën e mirë (Good night), Faleminderit (Thank you), Sa kushton kjo? (How much does this cost?) Ku është_____? (Where is___?). Besides, English language in not widely used especially among the older generation, but, almost everyone speaks fluent or at least knows a little Italian.

Note that you might get confused by their gestures when they approve or reject something. Smile and nod has different connotations in Albania. Albanians shake their heads left to right to mean "yes" and nod their heads up and down to express "no", which is the opposite to the rest of the world. Another gesture that Albanians use frequently and you may find it confusing is placing the palm on the chest. This specific gesture expresses gratitude, a way Albanians say thanks.

Also note that it is not allowed to go topless or naked in the public beaches along the coast, of course, there are many isolated places where you can do it in private. Homosexuality is decriminalized and the capital city - Tirana has few gay friendly bars and numerous LGBT support groups. Anti-discrimination and anti-hate laws are on point and penalties for drug-related crimes are severely punished.

Safety in Albania

If you like most of the people you are worried about the safety in Albania and you also have watched *Taken,* you should know that the violent crime rarely affects the travelers. However, it is worth being aware of the questionable driving habits of the locals and the high road accident rate. Otherwise, it is pretty safe to travel around Albania with most locals being hospitable and welcoming.

Harassment on the streets especially of women rarely occurs. However, pickpocketing does sometimes happen (significantly less than other major European destinations such as Paris or Barcelona). Therefore, always put your belongings in a safe place and be aware of your surroundings including on public transport. Also note that you may be overcharged in taxis, or bars and stores especially when costs for food and drink in Albania are generally low (except for some parts of the Riviera and the capital). Also, you may come across some suspicious sellers that will try to convince you to buy items such as expensive brand purses, watches, glasses or cell-phones and photo cameras. Do not pay attention to that, as most of that stuff is fake or stolen.

TRAVELLING TO ALBANIA

Plan your trip

Now that you are familiarized with the background information about Albania and its culture, it is the time to start planning your trip.

Planning a trip can be time-consuming and overwhelming, especially if you are travelling with kids. However, whether you are travelling alone or planning a family trip, you deserve to have a wonderful trip and make remarkable memories. This particular chapter will guide your through specific information you need to take into account before travelling to Albania.

Entry Requirements – Visa

Visa policy of Albania is based on the by Law Nr. 108/2013 "On foreign citizens", amended and the Decision of the Council of Ministers Nr. 513/2013 "On criteria and procedures for entry, stay and treatment of foreign citizens".

According to Albanian laws, a foreigner who intends to enter, stay, exit, or pass transit to / from the Republic of Albania must obtain a visa from one of the Albanian diplomatic missions. These missions can also provide you the further necessary information about Albania and entry requirements.

Visa policy of Albania is similar to the visa policy of the Schengen Area and you will not need a visa if you come from a visa exempt country or qualified for visa-free entry. All the foreigners who have a valid multi – entry Schengen visa, type "C" or "D", or a valid residence permit in one of the Schengen member states, can enter, stay and transit Albania without visa, within the validity term of the visa or the residence permit. Albania grants 90-day visa-free entry to all Schengen Annex II nationalities (Check out the link for the Schengen Visa Policy https://ec.europa.eu/home-affairs/what-we-do/policies/borders-and-visas/visa-policy_en), except for Dominica, East Timor, Grenada, Kiribati, Marshall Islands, Micronesia, Palau, Saint Lucia, Saint Vincent and the Grenadines, Samoa, Solomon Islands, Tonga, Tuvalu and Vanuatu. It also grants visa-free entry to several additional countries – Armenia, Azerbaijan, Kazakhstan, Kosovo, Kuwait and Turkey.

The visitor must be presented at the border crossing point and have a travel document (passport) recognized by the Republic of Albania with a validity term at least 3 months from the date of the arrival. Nationals of some countries and territories are allowed to enter Albania with valid ID cards *in lieu* of their passports.

(Check out the link for the list of countries and the specific requirements http://punetejashtme.gov.al/wp-content/

uploads/2018/11/3-visa-regime-for-foreign-citiznes-01.11.2018.pdf).

Public Transportation

All international arrivals enter through Mother Teresa International Airport which is the only airport in Albania and is located in Rinas, 17 km northwest of Tirana. Many tourists who travel to Albania and particularly the Southern part will fly into the airport of Corfu in Greece, which is just a short boat ride from Saranda in Albania. There are currently no direct flights to Saranda or Ksamil, but it's very easy to get from Corfu to Albania by the daily ferries.

However, there are many international flights to Tirana, the capital of Albania, and if you're visiting the northern part or go to Durrës it will be quicker and smoother to fly into Tirana.

Once you have landed in Tirana, go straight the shuttle bus service station - Tirana Rinas Express, to avoid the overpriced taxi fares which come to approximately 2,500 leke (20 euros) one way. The shuttle bus is way cheaper; the approximate cost is around 250 leke (2 euros), connects the airport with the city centre, near Scanderbag Square and takes about 20 minutes to arrive.

If you come from a country which has an accurately organized public transportation, and you are used to exact timetables where the trains, metros, trams or buses do not delay or at least you are updated with the changes, you should know and be prepared that this is not the case in Albania. So, forget your way of using public transport in your country.

Cities in Albania including the capital city Tirana do not have central bus stations, nor do they have travel agencies that work with the bus companies. Buses and *furgons* (privately run minibuses) are the main form of intercity transport in Albania.

As per buses, in Tirana there 3 main departure points, and the main routes are as following:

1) Southbound: From Tirana to:

1. Durrës - Every 30 min from 6:30AM to 7:30PM.

2. Fier - Every 30 min from 6:30AM to 5:30PM.

3. Vlorë - Every 30 min from 5.30AM to 5:30PM.

4. Himarë - 6:15AM, 1PM (8:30 PM also during summer).

5. Berat - Every 30 min from 6:30 AM to 5:30 PM.

6. Tepelenë - 11AM, 1PM, 2PM.

7. Gjirokastër - 6:45AM, 8AM, 9AM, 10AM, 11AM, 12AM, 1PM, 2:30PM, 3:30PM, 6:30PM.

8. Sarandë - 7AM, 8AM, 9:30AM, 10:30AM, 12:30PM, 4 PM.

9. Përmet - 6:30AM, 7:30AM, 12:30AM, 2PM, 5PM.

Southbound buses depart from South Interurban Station at Dogana.

2) Northbound: From Tirana to:

1. Shkoder - 7AM, 8 AM, 9 AM, 10 AM, 11 AM, 11:45AM, 12:30AM, 1:15PM, 2PM, 2:45PM, 3:30PM, 4:15PM, 5PM.

2. Kruje - 10AM, 11AM, 1PM, 3PM, 5PM, 6PM.

3. Kukes - 7AM, 9AM, 11AM, 1PM, 4PM, 6PM.

4. Pershkopi - 6AM, 8AM, 10AM, 11AM, 1PM, 2 PM, 4 PM, 5 PM.

5. Bajram Curri - 6AM, 8AM, 10AM, 12AM, 2PM.

Northbound buses depart from North Bus Terminal.

3) Southeast: From Tirana to:

1. Elbasan - Every 30 min from 6 AM to 8 PM

2. Pogradec - Every hour from 7:30 AM to 4:30 PM

3. Korcë - Every hour from 6:30 AM to 5:30 PM

4. Ersekë - 6AM, 10AM, 2:30 PM.

Southeast buses depart from “Qytet Studenti” station.

On the other hand, you will see the *furgons* everywhere, or at least hear the drivers calling out 'Durres, Durres' or 'Shkoder, Shkoder' depending on the city they are heading to. They operate independently of the bus network and they don't have timetables, instead they depart whenever all the seats are filled with passengers. Also, they do not have set fares; you have to negotiate it with the driver. However, the fares are low, and you either pay the conductor on board or when you hop off, which can be anywhere along the route. While buses and furgons are always cheap, the journeys can sometimes be quite long, so keep this in mind if you need to get somewhere in a hurry. They will even pick you up along the highway. Lately, there was an attempt to eliminate the furgons since they are not legal however, unsuccessful; you can still find them everywhere.

Finally, for those who want to see beautiful parts of Albania without taking any risks, I would recommend to take the highways between the big cities, along the coast and also the new road through Kelmend valley, which is an example of good infrastructure!

And for those who are ready for a great adventure: go ahead, discover the hidden places, enjoy the magnificent nature – you will not regret it!

Trains are not widely used in Albania, as the infrastructure is not quite good. However, many lines were renovated and there some trains in daily service with really low prices.

If you want an easier, faster and more comfortable way to tour around Albania, you can consider renting a car. However, many roads in Albania are in poor condition. If you are planning to only visit the big cities and the coastal areas you will not be facing any problems. But, if you want to enjoy all the stunning beauties of the country, you will have to use many different types of roads: highways, modern four-lane motorways, local roads full of holes and bumps, roads "under construction". On all roads, the highways as well as the local ones, you may see cattle, flocks of sheep with their shepherd, villagers on horse carts, people quietly riding donkeys and mules. Also, if you use GPS navigation, be aware that roads can also be poorly marked outside of Tirana and off the few main highways; sometimes they can be written only in Albanian or not at all.

Travelling to nearby Balkan countries

If you have rented a car and want to see other neighbouring countries know that as Balkan

countries are small, within a matter of few hours you will be able to reach the borders. However, if you are not travelling by car, do not worry there are plenty of other ways to travel to or from neighbouring countries. There are no international trains to or from Albania but you can always find a range of transport such as bus, taxi or ferry.

Travelling from Tirana to Bar (Montenegro), Podgorica (Montenegro) and Belgrade (Serbia)

- Firstly, take the afternoon train from Tiranë to Shkodër and stay overnight. Take bus if not running.

- On day 2, you have two options: Travel by taxi via the Han i Hotit border to Podgorica in Montenegro, or travel by bus to Ulcinj then another bus to Bar in Montenegro.

- If you choose the taxi option, the total journey from Shkodër to Podgorica is 59.7 km, and should take about 90 minutes including the need to change taxis at the border. Each of the two taxis should cost in the region of € 20.

- If you choose the bus option, there are three buses a day from Shkodër to Ulcinj in Montenegro via the Muriqan border crossing, at the time of writing these were 09:00, 14:15 & 16:00 (in the other direction, buses leave Ulcinj for Shkodër at 06:00, 12:30 and 16:30). There are then reasonably frequent buses from Ulcinj to Bar.

- Alternatively, a taxi from Shkodër to the border at Muriqan should cost about 10 – 15 €, and a taxi from Muriqan to Ulcinj around 20 – 25 €.

▪ Two daily trains link Bar and Podgorica with Belgrade, one a daytime train, the other an overnight sleeper with sleeping-cars and seats. The sleeper train will save you time as you can leave in the evening of the second day and arrive to Belgrade on the morning of third day. But staying the evening of day 3).

▪ In the other direction for travel to Albania, you can simply reverse the steps shown above.

Travelling from Tirana to Skopje (Macedonia)

▪ The easiest way to reach Skopje directly from Tirana is via bus. You have buses at 9: 00 AM, 16: 00 PM and 21: 00 PM. The journey should take you about 7 - 8 hours and the round way price is about 30 euros.

▪ Another way to reach Skopje is by firstly travelling to Pogradec. If you also want to take your time to visit the beautiful city of Pogradec, take the daily morning train from Tirana to Pogradec and stay overnight. Note that Pogradec station is about 2 km away from Pogradec town.

▪ Day 2, take a taxi from Pogradec to the border and on to Sveti Naum just the other side in Macedonia.

▪ Take another taxi or bus from Sveti Naum to Ohrid, journey about 1 hour.

▪ There are fairly frequent buses between Ohrid and Skopje.

Ferries from Albania to Bari or Ancona (Italy)

Check out the following links:

Tirrenia Line (formerly Adriatica Line) www.tirrenia.it

(Bari-Durrës daily, several per week Ancona-Durrës) and

www.agoudimos-lines.com (3-5 sailings a week Bari-Durrës), www.venezialines.com (fast ferry).

For onward trains within Italy see www.trenitalia.com.

Buses from Tirana to Athens and Thessaloniki (Greece)

- There are at least two daily buses between Tirana and Thessaloniki in Greece and the price is 30 euros one-way.
- Departures from Tirana are at 05:00 am or 08:15 am. The journey is usually long and takes about 11 hours.
- From Thessaloniki to Athens you can take a comfortable train and you will arrive there in about 5 hours.
- When travelling back to Tirana try to book from ktelmacedonia.gr/en/routes/&tid=43to
- Departures from Thessaloniki are at 09:00 am and 08:30 pm.

Accommodation

Even though Albania does not have a high tourist flow, yet, you will find a sufficient selection of clean and good hotels. Depending on where you are heading to, there is a range of accommodation: from luxurious hotels to more affordable hostels and apartment rooms which only charge around 10 to 15 euros per person, and all have most of the facilities and the free Wi-Fi. You will be able to find a double room with included breakfast for under €30 (prices are almost always quoted in euros). There are not usually any set rates for rooms, but if you ask for, you can also expect a small discount. Note that the prices differ depending on the season you are visiting. During the high season in summer the prices are higher and it will be better if you book ahead for private rooms on the coast.

Generally, the prices of the hotels are as below:

Average hotel price in Albania is: 5,126 ALL; 47 USD; 41 EURO;

Hostels prices in Albania are around: 1,593 ALL; 15 USD; 13 EURO;

Price of 1 star hotel in Albania is around: 3,565 ALL; 32 USD; 29 EURO;

Price of 2 stars hotel in Albania is around: 4,297ALL; 39USD; 35 EURO;

Price of 3 stars hotel in Albania is around: 4,778 ALL; 44 USD; 38 EURO;

Price of 4 stars hotel in Albania is around:6,641 ALL; 61 USD4; 53 EURO;

Price of 5 stars hotel in Albania is around:9,059 ALL; 83 USD; 73 EURO;

Top Luxury Hotels in Albania

- The Plaza Tirana
- Xheko Imperial Hotel
- Rogner Hotel Tirana
- Prestige Resort
- Hotel Boutique LAS

- E.K.A Luxury Penthouse 2
- MAK Albania Hotel
- Mondial Boutique Hotel
- Privilege Hotel and Spa
- Elysium Hotel
- Hotel Hymeti Palace
- Adriatik Hotel
- Hotel Flower and SPA
- The Rooms Hotel and Residence

Budget Hotels

Generally Albania has many classy hotels that cost less than those in the rest of Europe. During the summer season the hotels have higher prices, but you can always find an apartment, especially along the coastal areas. Most of the apartments are very cheap in the shoulder season and reasonable during summer.

However, if you would prefer a hotel instead of apartment, here is a category of the budget hotels, aiming to make it easier for the budget travelers to choose economic accommodation in Albania. The budget hotels stated in this section are selected from different locations and Albanian towns. The budget hotels in the capital city of Tirana are a bit more expensive than budget hotels in other towns but are still very reasonably priced compared to budget hotels in European capital cities. Have a look at the list below to find some of the most affordable accommodation in Albania:

- Panorama (Zaharia, Kruje)
- Sirena (Tushemisht, Pogradec)
- Te Stela Resort (Highway Tirana – Durres)
- Rezidenca Desaret (Kala, Berat)
- Kolping (Shkodra)

- Nais (Durres)
- Europa (Tirana)
- Alpin (Tirana)
- Green (Tirana)
- Boci (Elbasan)
- Lot Boutique Hotel (Tirana)
- Tirana Backpacker Hostel (Tirana)
- Destil Hostel (Tirana)
- Rapsodia (Shengjin)

Campsites

If you are a backpacker and want to take the budget travelling to whole another level, you might consider camping. If you enjoy camping and can manage without facilities there are also few beautiful campsites located all over the country, and along the beaches of the Ionian coast.

Some of the best campsites are as following:

- Camping Riviera Shengjin
- Camping Clandestino, Velipoja
- Camping Elvis, Fier
- Hotel Camping Mali i Robit, Golem
- Camping Jale
- Vuno Camping
- Gate to Horizon Bio Camping Lukova
- Kamping Himara

- One Way Camping Qeparo
- Star Camp, Qeparo
- Camper Beach Baro, Orikum Vlora
- Camping Llogara
- Kolektiv Camping Drymades, Dhermi
- Camping Olive Garden, Dhermi

CURRENCY & PRICES

THE NATIONAL CURRENCY IN ALBANIA IS THE ALBANIAN **LEKË** (ALL) which is also often used in its singular form, lek. Coins of 1, 5, 10, 20, 50 and 100 lekë are in circulation, as are notes of 200, 500, 1000, 2000 and 5000 lekë. The Bank of Albania publishes the value of the Albanian currency against foreign currencies. For daily official exchange rates, please visit the site of the National Bank of Albania. However, usually the exchange rate for 1 euro is around 125 lekë, and for 1 dollar is 110 lekë. Exchange offices are the best places to change money, and can be found in most cities.

The banks are open from Monday to Friday; from 8.00 am to 3.30 pm. ATMs as well are widely available in most towns. Credit cards such are usually accepted in banks in Tirana and the main hotels, restaurants and shops, and every year their usage becomes more widespread. American Express, MasterCard are generally accepted, however, it is best to find out from your bank before you leave.

Albania is a relatively inexpensive travel destination when compared to other European countries. Within the Balkan

Peninsula the country holds an average price level. Greece and Montenegro are more expensive options for travellers. In a global comparison, Albania is not an expensive destination. However, the prices differ depending where you are heading to. In the Southern tourist resorts such as Ksamil and Saranda, the prices will be higher than the country's average, and villages without tourism will be cheaper than the average.

Note that, out of the habit the many sellers haven't yet caught up with the chopping off of a zero. They still use the old money currency when telling you the prices. For example for an item that costs 100 lekë the seller will tell you it costs 1000 lekë. Don't forget to ask whether the price is with the old or the new money.

Accommodation prices are quoted in euros at all but the cheapest places, and some of the more supermarket restaurants do likewise; in these you can pay with either currency, though will usually save a little paying in lekë.

Below, you can see the average prices of some products and services we use in our daily lives:

FOOD

Daily menu in the business district 668 ALL /4.75 EUR

Combo meal in fast food restaurant (Big Mac Meal or similar) 439.84 ALL / 3.19 EUR

1 bottle of red table wine, good quality (Middle Range)

600 ALL / 4.35 EUR

2 liters of Coca-Cola 175 ALL / 1.24 EUR

A loaf of fresh white bread (500g) 61 ALL / 0.49 EUR

Water (1.5 liter bottle) 52 ALL / 0.42EUR

CLOTHES

1 summer dress in a chain store (Zara, H&M, ...) 4,916.52 ALL / 35.62 EUR

1 pair of Nike trainers 8,256.64 ALL / 59.82 EUR

1 pair of average business shoes 7.965.60 ALL / 57.71 EUR

PERSONAL CARE

Deodorant, roll-on (50ml ~ 1.5 oz.) 375 ALL / 2.67 EUR

4 rolls of toilet paper 160 ALL /1.14 EUR

Standard men's haircut in expat area of the city 450 ALL /3.2 EUR

FURTHER USEFUL INFORMATION

Emergency and important numbers in Albania

The country code for Albania is +355. Roaming for the tourist is provided by Amc Mobil, Eagle Mobile, Plus and Vodafone.

Here is a list of the emergency numbers in Albania, in case you need them.

Emergency service Number

Road police 126

Ambulance 127

Fire brigade 128

State Police 129

General emergency 112

Emergency at sea 125

Tirana's central hospital +355 4 234 9209

Night pharmacy 04/22 222 41

Links/ websites for important information

Government Offices Hours of Operation: 08.00-16.30, from Monday to Friday. If you need further information during your stay in Albania, there are a few tourist information offices dotted around, though hours can be irregular to say the least – they can supply maps and book accommodation, but you're better off asking for information at your hotel or hostel.

Ministry of Tourism, Culture, Youth and Sports

Tel: 00 355 4 2232488

Website: www.mtkrs.gov.al

National Tourism Organization

Tel/Fax: 00 355 4 2273281

Accommodation - booking rooms online

www.albania-hotel.com

Collection of historical/cultural articles

www.albanianhistory.net

CUISINE & SHOPPING

EVEN THOUGH ALBANIA MAY BE A LITTLE COUNTRY, AT ONLY 11 square miles and with a total population of three around million people, yet there is a lot to do and see in this exciting location. Albania's long breathtaking coastline is one of the most beautiful in the world. From the stunning beaches of the Albanian Riviera to the attractive archaeological sites, you certainly will not be disappointed. There are so many reasons why you should visit Albania. It is a country that is truly unique and authentic. Around every twist and turn, you will find another beautiful landscape or beach. The people are extremely friendly and very hospitable. It is a unique European country with strong traditions and culture.

This little country lately is becoming more popular destination for tourists, yet it remains extremely little-known and unspoiled. One of the main concerns of everyone travelling to a new destination is the places they should visit. Albania has many great cities, towns and villages that you should not miss out on when you come to visit. Albania boasts some of the best examples of Ottoman architecture in the world, along with clear Mediterranean air and lovely beaches.

And, perhaps best of all, travelling to Albania remains an extremely affordable trip, even compared to the rest of this part of Europe. Therefore, in this particular Chapter, I have named some of the best places to visit in Albania that you should visit during your time here, food you should try, things you should do, outdoor activities you should not miss, so on and so forth.

From picturesque villages to lovely cities and beach towns – there is something for everyone coming to Albania. So, let's have a look at the best things that Albania has is store for you!

The Albanian Cuisine

The Albanian cuisine is a demonstration of the hospitality of the people, whose love for their guests and their effort to treat them in the best possible way is renowned. Albanians are devoted cooks, chefs, culinary experts and general food and pleasure enthusiasts. Preparing a nice meal, enjoying fresh foods, being exceptionally gracious hosts, and giving in to life's simple pleasures are important for any Albanian.

The Albanian cuisine is the national cuisine of the Albanian people which generally is considered to be Mediterranean, with influences from Italian, Greek and Turkish cuisines. Its position gives it a rare advantage as this country has only delicious influences from all sides. It is characterized by the use of Mediterranean herbs such as oregano, mint, basil, rosemary and more in cooking meat and fish, but also chilli pepper and garlic. Also, lots of importance is laid upon fruits and vegetables. Almost every Albanian recipe contains vegetables of what is seasonal and available.

In high elevation localities, smoked meat and pickled preserves are common. Dairy products are integral part of the cuisine usually accompanied with ever present bread and alcoholic beverages such as Raki. Seafood specialties are also common in the coastal cities such as Durrës, Vlorë, Shkodër, Lezhë and Sarandë.

The Albanian food is authentic, delicious and can be found all around the country with really affordable prices. Albanians generally try to combine taste with foods which have nutritional value. The most important meal for Albanians is lunch, and it is usually a home cooked stew, slowly cooked meat with different veggies and a salad of fresh seasonal vegetables. Whatever type of food you prefer, Albanian food has enough of a variety to satisfy all your food cravings while travelling around the country.

Besides, Albania has also a serious café culture almost unlike anywhere else you have ever been. The day or any work for Albanians starts only after they have had their first cup of coffee in the morning. For Albanians their coffee is as important as the tea is for English or Turkish people. You can find beautiful and cozy cafés in every corner; they pay attention a lot to their decorations as well as services. The prices are cheap, only about 0.50 cents per cup. Thus, within any time throughout the day, you will see the cafés are full of people sitting, sipping coffee and socializing. Additionally, this cafe culture is completed with "dolces" (sweets or desserts in Italian) which are very popular in Albania. People sit in cafes while puffing on cigarettes, drinking espresso and eating these delicious desserts. And you can't just quickly drink a cup and move on. You sit, you chat, and you do not rush or hurry. This is a huge part of Albanian café culture.

12 Must-Try Albanian Foods

FLIJA

Flija also known as *fli* or *flia,* is one of the most favored dish in Albanian and Kosovo Albanian cuisine It consists of multiple pancake layers brushed with cream and baked slowly within few hours. It takes only a few simple ingredients to make it such as (flour, butter, oil, yoghurt, water and salt) however; this delicious dish depends on your baking skills so its preparation involves hard, painstaking work.

What makes this dish special is that each layer is baked separately with with a *saç* (which is a spherical metal lid that is placed over a pan that sits on what's best to describe it, a BBQ on the ground). Using a traditional saç the key is to keep the temperature consistent. An open BBQ would be made on the ground and when ready the Flija will be made in a large pan / baking tray that is place directly onto it, while the next layer is being added the saç will be covered with ashes from the ground BBQ to bring and keep it at a steady temperature.

It is prepared for celebration of births, weddings or other auspicious ceremonies; you can have it for lunch time or any time of the day. It is served with honey, or yogurt or *kaymak* (crème) even pickled vegetables, jam and cheese. Also, March 18 is recognized as the Flija Day in which families invite their relatives for preparing and eating Flija.

BYREK

Byrek is baked vegetable pie with a thin, layered, flaky phyllo pastry that can be filled with various ingredients such as spinach and cheese, mashed potatoes, cabbage, tomatoes, other veggies or minced meat. It is crispy and flaky at the exterior, soft and creamy within, the taste varying according to the ingredients added. Similar versions of byrek you can find all over other Balkan countries. Another version of the byrek is served as a filling for "pite" or "pita". In some countries byrek or burek is the same as pita, while in the others consider as byrek only those filled with meat, and everything else is pita.

Byrek is really delicious and it is eaten typically for breakfast commonly accompanied with tea or with ayran (a salty yogurt drink). Even though it is most popular breakfast of the locals, for you byrek might be little oily and heavy in the morning.

If you visit the UNESCO site, the city of Berat, head towards the Mangalemi Restaurant (a traditional restaurant, with authentic home cooked Albanian food) and try their special Byrek Mangalemi the savoury byrek filled with fluffy mix of pumpkin, potato, cottage cheese and a hint of lemon.

. . .

TAVE KOSI (TAVE ELBASANI)

Tave kosi is a soured milk casserole, one of the most favorite national dishes in Albania, especially in the city of Elbasan, and is also named after this city. It is also known in the Turkey cuisine as Elbasan tava, but they usually use Béchamel sauce instead of the traditional and original yoghurt and eggs topping.

As much as Albanians love vegetables, their cuisine features lamb and beef as well. Tave kosi is a dish of lamb meat and rice baked in a clay or ceramic pot with a mixture of eggs and yoghurt (instead of the original soured milk). Sometimes, as an alternative to the lamb meat, chicken meat is used and it is called *tave kosi me mish pule* (tave kosi with chicken meat). It has a delicious savoury taste, with warm meat and light, creamy egg topping.

QOFTE

Qofte or *Kofta* is a dish spread all over the Middle Eastern Balkan, as well as South and Central Asian cuisine and one of the favorite dishes of the locals in Albania. They are seasoned and grilled meatballs or meatloaves consisting of the minced or ground meat (generally beef, lamb, pork or chicken or some combination) mixed with spices, aromatic herbs, onions and several vegetables. Depending on the place you try them, they are made of different meats, yet, qofte in Albania is made of mixing beef and lamb. In special places, an alternative for the vegetarians include qoftes made from potatoes or squash.

Qofte is usually known as fast food, as a type of kebab and in

Albania it is served with raw onion, bread and spicy peppers. You also can have it with salads, yogurt or bread for lunch or dinner. It is soft enough to melt in your mouth, with the addition of herbs making it aromatic. If you have it with a dip of yogurt, then it would be a perfect blend of salty and sour. Some places in Albania known as *Qofteri* specialize in selling qofte as well as beer. You can always tell when there's a Qofteri in the nearby area serving qofte, because the smell of grilled meat will find you before you find it!

ALBANIAN MIXED GRILL

Albanians love meat, thus, everywhere across Albania, you will find grill houses or as Albanians refer to, *zgara*. One of the most popular meals is a big plate of mixed grilled meat, typically ordered with a salad, some grilled vegetables and an assortment of dips, sauces and spreads with this meal, and everyone digs in family style. Grilled vegetables are a popular appetizer or accompaniment not only in Albanian food, but all of the eastern Balkans. Typically, eggplant, zucchini, tomatoes, onions and peppers are the vegetables of choice, and oftentimes cheese will be crumbled on top.

Finally, at the end of nearly every meal, you are usually served (oftentimes without being asked) a small glass of *raki*. Raki is very similar, if not the same as rakia, which is found all over the Balkans. Raki (a) is a fruit brandy drink with an alcohol content of 40%, though often homemade raki has a higher alcohol content, sometimes much higher. It is made of fruits such as plums or grapes and is typically clear unless it's been aged in wooden barrels. While it goes down like fire, it's a typical way to end an Albanian meal, and after a few times, you almost start to get used to it.

. . .

FËGESË

This simple dish's main ingredients are green and red bell peppers, along with skinned tomatoes and onions which are cooked down with cottage cheese and seasoned with a whole lot of spices and finally baked to make a thick texture. It is smooth and tastes cheesy and creamy, and you can have it for lunch with bread or side dish. When accompanied with some bread is actually quite filling.

Although the traditional version of *fërgesë* is purely vegetarian, in the present times you can find places that also use lamb or beef for its preparation.

KAÇKAVAL

Kaçkaval (or kashkavall) can be found, in one way or another, all over the Balkans. The term is often used generically to describe yellow cheese, but in this instance, it refers to pan-fried cheese. The cheese is salty, and when fried, it is melting and delicious and goes really well with beer. Definitely not the healthiest option on the menu, but one of the most delicious ones for sure.

Kaçkaval is often used within the Albanian-style meze platters that also include prosciutto ham, salami and feta cheese, accompanied with roasted bell peppers (capsicum) or green olives marinated in olive oil with garlic or onions.

SPECA TE MBUSHURA (STUFFED PEPPERS)

A typical appetizer or vegetable dish in Albania is a stuffed pepper. Most of Eastern European countries cook a version of stuffed peppers with minced meat or ground beef and rice. In Albania as well, the stuffed peppers are usually filled with ground, rice, tomatoes, onions an array of vegetables and delicious Mediterranean spices. It is really delicious and a healthy choice too.

Another alternative of stuffed peppers is *speca me gjize* (peppers stuffed with cottage cheese). Yellow, orange or red peppers are stuffed with rice, cottage cheese and spices, before being baked in the oven. This was one of the favorite appetizers for the locals

FRESHLY CAUGHT SHRIMP

If you love seafood, know that you can find really delicious and fresh specialties in the coastal cities of Albania. Especially in Saranda, being located right on the Ionian Sea, it comes as no surprise that fresh seafood is popular with tourists and locals there. The fishermen sell their catch early in the morning right along the pedestrian promenade, so if you want to take a peek at the fish on offer, head there around 9:00 and check it out. Dining seaside while feasting on freshly caught shrimp is a must-try in Albania!

. . .

SALLATE SHOPE

One of the most widespread salads in Albania, especially during the summer is the *sallate shope,* the simple salad made of cucumbers, tomatoes, onions and cheese salad. It's sometimes served with olives, sometimes with corn, but always with cucumbers, tomatoes, onions and cheese. When the ingredients are this fresh not much else is needed, but, you can dress your salad with olive oil, salt and pepper, and sometimes a squeeze or lemon or a bit of vinegar.

SHËNDETLI

One of the most popular and delicious desserts in Albania, is *shendetli.* It is a honey nut cake made with all of the usual cake suspects – baking soda, flour, sugar, eggs. However, what makes it special and delicious this dessert is the addition of the honey and walnuts.

Also, when the cake is ready, hot syrup made with vanilla, sugar, water and cloves is poured over the cake and left to soak overnight. This dessert is delicious, and isn't too sweet either.

KABUNI

Another traditional dessert is *kabuni* which is prepared by frying rice in butter, caramelized sugar, mutton broth (ram's neck only) and seasoning it with ground cloves, sugar, cinnamon, raisins, and almond once boiled. The end product is a baked rice pudding, mostly served cold. It tastes delicious and is grainy and crispy, while the addition of garnishes intensifies its sweet taste.

. . .

The best places to eat traditional Albanian food

As in many other countries in the Mediterranean and Balkan region, the traditional cuisine in Albania is really tasty and diverse. Until a couple of years ago, Albanians would have preferred advertising their skill at perfectly cooking foreign dishes to their own, not knowing that their own traditional cuisine stands out and it is a real treasure. However, lately since realizing the importance of their own traditional cuisine, countless amazing, traditional restaurants have opened which demonstrate this tradition. Tipping in restaurants is appreciated (10% is normal) and expected in fancier places. While, in bars and cafés it will be polite to leave some change.

While you can find hundreds of places that serve delicious traditional food in Albania – and, as Albanians love to say, "one is better than the other" – here in this section you will only find the very best places. So, without any further ado, let's have a look at some of the places where you will have the most delightful meals and feel the warm and cozy atmosphere that is so inherently Albanian.

Mullixhiu

You can find this restaurant stated in any list of recommendations of places to eat in Tirana. It has been named as Tirana's Best Hospitality and Fine Dining. This traditional restaurant has won the heart of locals as well as the tourists. It has beautiful wooden, rustic environment, and their menu is full with fresh and most traditional Albanian meals. Most importantly, this place won hearts of every Albanian as it is the only place in the city that serves trahana. Trahana is a traditional dish in Albanian cuisine that refers to a dough or powder made using various vegetables, spices, yeast, and yogurt. The name can refer to the actual powder or dough itself, as well as a soup made by using the dough or powder and adding boiling water. The charming and the famous chef of this restaurant, Bledar Kola won 3rd place in the World Gourmet Society Best Plate amongst many talented chefs in Monte Carlo by preparing this staple Albanian dish.

Restaurant Oda

This small traditional restaurant is one of the ten recommended restaurants in Tirana. Located, right next to the hopping *Pazari i Ri* (new market) neighborhood, you can find this beautiful place. It casts a light on Ottoman culinary influences present in Albanian cuisine, and invites its visitors to discover perhaps the best traditional-style restaurant in Tirana. *Oda* has an authentic old house location and its name Oda refers to the small rooms inside the traditional Ottoman homes in Tirana and the interior is decorated that way that resembles a traditional room with low ceilings and low tables as well as traditional carpets adorning the floor. Small, but unforgettable! The food is as authentic, delicious and very inexpensive, featuring roasted lamb, byrek, fërgesë, pllaqi, and so much more. You will also find the best selection of homemade raki here.

Sofra e Ariut

Sofra e Ariut is one of the most prestigious restaurants in the city of Tirana in Albania. Albanian traditional cuisine, waiter's local outfits, frames with ethnographic reach clothing from different regions of Albania give a characteristic and unique feeling to every person who visits this place. You can find one of the best "Tavë Kosi" and "Fërgesa Tiranase" as well as with grape raki "Sofra e Ariut." In 2011 at the event L'IMPERO DEI SAPORI INTERNAZIONALI, won the hearts of the international jury also awarded first prize for outstanding taste and unique that brings these dishes.

Ceni's

It is located near the Artificial Lake of Tirana and is known as the beat meat place in town, especially their steaks and veal. This restaurant does not only prepare traditional Albanian dishes, but it is a mixture of the Italian cuisine too. The meats and poultry are cooked in Albanian-style while the homemade pasta rivals are cooked in Italian- style. This restaurant this restaurant proves that the best things come in small packages it is great at dish-wine pairings, probably the best you'll find in Tirana. Therefore, this has become one of those well-kept places that you should not be missing.

Bujtina e Gjelit

Built in 1992, this hotel-restaurant-bar is located in the legendary neighborhood of Don Bosko in Tirana. You need a good reason to visit this area and *Bujtina e Gjelit* (Guesthouse of the Rooster) is it. This guesthouse is masterfully built in traditional materials of iron, stone and wood. Most products served in the restaurant come from the "Gjeli Farm" and are purely fresh and organic. Using oven brick ovens and traditional equipment, the menu has a tasty selection of meats: rotisserie piglet, oven baked lamb, ember cooked sausages, byrek (traditional baked pie, see above), are only some of the specialties here.

UKA Farm

Located just outside Tirana, near the Mother Theresa International Airport, this farm-to-table restaurant is one of the must-sees in Tirana. The long, cool vineyards and the modern and open space of the dining area makes this a pretty great spot to relax after your plane lands, before you make it to the bustling city. Opened in 1996, this restaurant is run by a great young chef and winemaker, named Flori Uka. Their specialties include their wonderful homemade wine, cheese stuffed pickled peppers, lamb and locally made cheese, and much more. What you'll notice is the freshness in everything you taste!

Ceren Ismet Shehu

Outside of Tirana, in the small village of Surrel in the Dajti Mountain, this restaurant serves traditionally Albanian food! Surrounded by turkeys and goats running around the beautiful hills of the village, this restaurant serves dishes not only in a traditional way, but in an antique way! Meat comes out in old iron skillets, raki in vintage vases, and everything smells of cherry pine. The fresh air and the warm atmosphere are worthy of a very long lunch or supper. Some of the best dishes are *flija e veriut* (the northern pie prepared with delicious meat broth), pickled tomatoes, raw pumpkin salad, *petka me hithra* (homemade Albanian pasta), as well as fresh, homemade cheese. Not enough can be said about this unlikely haven right next to the capital.

. . .

Reka Restaurant

A local favorite since it first opened in 2002, this restaurant has some of the best traditional Albanian cuisine and some of the most delicious dishes from the northern region of Dibra. In addition the meat, especially lamb, the two legendary plates to try here are *jüfka* (amazingly buttery, fluffy pasta) and the most delicious Albanian dessert *sheqerpare,* a melt-in-your mouth buttery, syrupy goodness. In Albanian *sheqer* means "sugar" so you can only imagine the sweetness level on this one.

Restaurant Mangalemi

This restaurant is located only 300 meters from the city centre (Mangalem Quarter) and very close to the historical sites of Berat. Traditional Berati architecture is reflected in the subtle combination of wood and stone and the dedication to detailed décor. The restaurant offers a range of choice from the Albanian tradition of cooking. In preparing the dishes, they select fresh products daily, organic when possible, at the local farmers' market. You will enjoy the carefully prepared traditional specialties. They also offer a long list of locally produced different kinds of raki. When it comes to wine, you will be able to find the best products from the city wineries. The restaurant offers 2 indoor spaces, 1 covered veranda (Çardak) and a terrace overlooking the city. Summer nights on its breezy veranda are not to be missed!

Mrizi i Zanave - Fishtë

Located near Lezhë, this farm-to-table restaurant and

vineyard has slowly become quite the legend among food enthusiasts and for good reason. Hailed as one of the most innovative, organic, authentically Albanian restaurants, this place has is packed on a daily basis so you have to make sure and make reservations. Do not skip on any of the dishes suggested by the waiters, they are not trying to sell you more but simply trying to make you realize how amazingly delicious this food is! The appetizers are to die for: fresh cheeses, fresh pomegranate juice, locally made jams and more. The meats, the best you may have ever had. The roasted kid and lamb cooked in milk are some of the equally traditional and exotic delicacies to choose from. You can also spend the night in one of their beautiful rooms so you can turn dinner into a relaxing food and wine tour!

Hotel Millenium - Tushemisht

Tushemisht, near the city of Pogradec, is one of the current hottest spots to visit in Albania, famous for its great lake panoramas and fresh food. Hotel Millennium, located right across from Lake Ohrid, is also very well-known for its restaurant which serves fresh, traditional Albanian cuisine. Their fërgesë, a traditional Albanian staple made of peppers cooked in a fresh tomato and feta cheese sauce, and their freshly made feta cheese are pretty amazing! But, the next best thing to the beautiful view is ther Ohrid trout stew, which is the best kind of fish soup you will ever taste.

Taverna Antoneta – Boboshticë

If you choose to go to the beautiful, mountainous village of Boboshticë near Korçë, this is the place that you should not miss visiting. Located among lush green gardens, famous people flock to this traditional tavern like bees to honey – they know this is the best food to be had in this area which, by the way, has no shortage of delicious food. Any meal is a feast at this family restaurant which has the best *lakror* (a more delicate version of the traditional spinach or meat – filled baked pie byrek), assortment of pickled peppers and tomatoes, usually stuffed with fresh gjizë, Albania's salty cottage cheese, and juicy meats.

Hotel Pashuta- Voskopojë

The fresh air, spectacular landscapes, fresh flowers that surround the great porch in Hotel Pashuta make this a heavenly place to enjoy the delicious dishes they serve. Located right outside Korçë and owned by a very warm and hospitable family, this place makes you feel at home as soon as you step in the door. Fresh organic food is prepared carefully and beautifully served in small portions of local delicacies including *pllaqi* salad (big juicy baked beans), trahana (a unique dish made of wheat, bread, olive oil and feta cheese), *petulla* (Albanian doughnuts), local fresh meats, and brick oven baked pies, all served with a very special blackberry raki.

Farma Sotira- Gërmenj

This place is for the adventurers out there and offers a once in a lifetime experience which includes camping, hiking, trout fishing, and more. Located within a beautiful pine forest on the side of a mountain, Farma Sotira is a working trout farm with several small log cabins, beautifully aligned along a meadow. The dining area built in stone rests right over the trout stream that runs through the farm and furnishes it with the most delicious, fresh fish you will get to taste! Fresh meat cooked in embers as well as homemade dairy products are some of the best things from this great list of traditional delicacies. The farm's homemade wine is amazing, too!

Shopping in Albania

Given the brief time since Albania moved from a communist economy to a free market, it is surprising how well regarded it is for commercialism, with Tirana at its helm. Those who would like to devote a whole day to shopping will enjoy how easy it is to get around the small capital as well as other towns. Sales associates are friendly, on the whole, and usually know their business.

The shopping hours are usually from 09:00 - 16:00 throughout the whole week (Monday-Sunday) and then again for a couple of hours in the early evening (variable according to the time of the year). Note that not all shops are open on Sundays.

If like most of the tourists you love buying souvenirs from the countries you are visiting, Albania will not disappoint you. There are plenty of souvenirs shops in all the towns, and especially in Tirana. In most of the historical places, you will also find souvenirs sold in the streets. Don't forget to bargain, you can get great discounts! As mentioned previously, note that you may come across some suspicious sellers that will try to convince you to buy items such as expensive brand purses, watches, glasses or cell-phones and photo cameras. Do not pay attention to that, as most of that stuff is fake or stolen.

In Tirana, there are some specific streets where you can find beautiful souvenirs, such as Myslym Shyri Street and continuing to Çam Street, as well as the place known as 9 kateshet (9-storey building on Barrikada Street). In all these shops you will find Albanian traditional folk costumes, as well as other artisanal products. Below you will find some of the best souvenir shops in Tirana:

Time Souvenir, Tradita Shqiptare which you will find at the st. Myslym Shyri, Tirana, Tel: 04 2270 858; 0693926143.

Nji Mar, Nji Mrapsht - You can find a variety of handmade gifts and accessories. You will find this place at the st. Kont Urani, Tirana. Here is also their Facebook page https://www.facebook.com/NjiMarNjiMrapsht/, Tel: 069 400 5542.

Rreli-Erebara- Traditional folk costumes from all over Albania, as well as wood, bronze and silver souvenirs, pottery, ceramics and antiques which you will find at st. Ded Gjo Luli, Tel +355 4 222 12 82.

Art Forever - If you're looking for folk costumes, antique chests, wood carvings, or old books, check out this one-man show. Find it near the corner of Blv. Bajram Curri, st. Vaso Pasha 99, Tel: +355 4 224 63 86.

Prodhime Bakri dhe Filigrami - There is plenty selection of the fridge magnets and a few antiques, and decorated teacups and small vases, decorated porcelain figurines, painted miniatures or photographs in stand-up frames reminding the Communist-era. You will find this shop near the Stephen Centre Café, st. Ibrahim Rugova, Sky Tower, Tel +355 69 20 910 07.

Pirro Souvenirs - A good selection of handicrafts and

souvenirs; Albanian flags, key rings, T-shirts, and must-have mugs depicting Enver Hoxha, King Zog and Mother Teresa among others. You will find it at st. Abdyl Frasheri tel: +355 4 222 55 87.

Adrion International Bookshop - If you love books or want to bring one as souvenir, you should visit this shop. It is located right in the heart of the city, within the Palace of Culture. This long-established bookshop has an excellent selection of books on Albania (including many in English) you're unlikely to find elsewhere, as well as good maps and a selection of guidebooks to the region. There's also a large selection of English-language novels and nonfiction titles, postcards and souvenirs.

Pazari i Ri – The New Market

Come here to witness Tirana's ebullient street life. Every day from dawn, traders come here to hawk fruit, vegetables, meat and fish, and whether you're actually looking to buy anything yourself or not, it's a wonderful place to stroll and soak up the atmosphere.

Recently given a massive facelift, the market is known as the New Market but is actually one of the oldest parts of the city. Some splendid and cheap restaurants and cafés ring the main market.

When it comes to clothing and brands you can find most of them in one of the malls within Tirana.

Universe Shopping Mall (QTU) was the first of it's the kind in Tirana since 2005. QTU is conveniently situated, just 6km from the city center along the busiest highway Tiranë –

Durrës. It offers a convenient setting for easy-access shopping. QTU remains a premier shopping destination with over 70 brands, restaurants and leisure activities for the entire family, and it continues to grow. From casual to modern fashion, dining, kids' entertainment, you will find everything for family shoppers in QTU, all in a one floor building. Tirana's very first shopping mall, QTU (Universe Commercial Center), has been in business since 2005 and still retains that original magic. When it first opened, it signaled a new era of commerce in Albania.

Tirana Ring Center it one of the most accessible shopping malls in Tirana. It is strategically located in one of the busiest part of Tirana, only 5 min from "Skënderbej" Square, at roundabout of "Zogu I Zi." It is one of the biggest shopping centre in Tirana and offers to its customers the pleasure of shopping and entertainment with a modern and innovative concept which brings a new shopping experience referring the European standards.. Tirana Ring Center brings to the Albanian consumers a wide range of over 70 brands, hypermarket, entertainment spaces, adorable restaurants and coffee bars and high comfort, food court, 4 parking floors (with over 500 parking spaces), 4,000 m2 offices, 50 apartments and 2 villas over the centre.

Tirana East Gate Mall is located about four kilometers from the city center, just off the national road Tirana-Elbasan, in Lundra region. Four bus lines connect the city with the Tirana East Gate which you will find in the city center near the Et'hem Bey Mosque. The Tirana East Gate operates since November 2011 and is about 90,000 square meters of retail space. The building has two storey and accommodates 180 shops, 10 bars cafes and 5 restaurants. Approximately 3,300 parking spaces are available. TEG is part of Balfin Group one of the biggest investor in Albania and in Balkans.

TOPTANI Shopping Mall - The closest shopping mall is the Toptani Shopping Center is the newest and the closest mall to the center, located only about 400 meters from the city center[the shopping center was inaugurated on 13 March 2017 and has about 12,790 m2 of retail space covering 7 floors above ground with four underground floors for parking. It accommodates 80 shops, 5 cafes, 2 restaurants and with approximately 600 parking spaces available.

CityPark Shopping Mall - Considered to be one of the most luxurious in Albania, this mall doubles as an amusement park for children and teens. CityPark, located along the Tiranë – Durrës Highway, includes brand stores, bars and restaurants, a skating rink, and the biggest AquaPark in the country, which opens only in during the summer.

Coin – Aba Business Center - The famous Italian department store COIN is part of the iconic ABA BUSINESS

CENTER tower, near the main boulevard of Tirana. With five levels of some of the most well-known brands in the world, COIN enjoys its reputation as Tirana's most glamorous shopping center.

ETC Gallery - The ETC Gallery is part of a residential building, famous for its architecture and location. Its stores, hypermarket, bars and restaurants, have made this center quite a popular hub if activity during the years.

Shopping Center Pazari Korça

Located at the Old Bazaar of the city of Korca, this shopping mall lends an otherwise very historical area a modern touch! With more than 60 commercial activities, it offers a wide range of shops and other services for all those who would like to leave the historical sights of Korçë behind for a few moments and enjoy the fruits of the 21st century.

TIRANA

TIRANA - THE HEART AND THE CAPITAL CITY OF ALBANIA. There are different thoughts regarding the origin of the name of the city. Some think that it relates to Tyrrenia (a name of Etruscan origins), while other believe that it relates to the word Theranda (harvest), or to the Tirkan (a castle at the foot of Mount Dajti).

Tirana cannot be described in just few words. It is one of the coolest cities in Europe and just like all other European metropolitan cities; it has never-ending movement and energy. Words such as colorful city or vibrant city are just an attempt to give some sort of impression of the culture, passion and enjoyment to be found in the city. Whether it is a visit in one of the attractions, museums and surrounding castles or an evening at clubs and bars in the trendiest parts of the city, you will definitely be inspired and surprised of the joys and experiences that Tirana has to offer.

With its clubs, bars, cafes, and taverns, Tirana is worth discovering by both day and night, as well as during both: the summer and the winter. In the summer as most people have drifted towards the beaches of Saranda or Durres and the city isn't as busy but in the winter the city is thriving again. There are lots of things to do in Tirana so I highly recommend spending a few days there.

Your own journey might begin by visiting the museums and the key spots such as Sheshi Skënderbej, where you will be able to see the Mosque of Et'hem Bey (built between 1798 and 1812) and the 35 m high Kulla e Sahatit (the Watch Tower), built in 1822 with a San Marco style cupola. Next, you can visit the famous mosaic uncovered on the floor of an old Roman lodge. Its center configures the walls of the castle of the Roman emperor Justinian (A.D. 520). The monumental Tomb of Kapllan Pasha and the Ura e Tabakëve (a bridge constructed in the beginning of the 19th century, located on Bulevardi Zhan D'Ark) are also worth visiting. You can also look at the old communist leader's house, Enver Hoxha. I highly recommend visiting the house of leaves, which is where you can find out a bit more about what Albania was like in the communist times.

As a capital, Tirana has the country's finest museums, theatres, and galleries representing the national arts. A visit to the National History Museum, the Archeological Museum, the Natural Science Museum, the private Mezuraj Museum, and the National Gallery of the Arts will leave wonderful memories. You can also pass a pleasant evening in the National Theatre or the Opera and Ballet Theatre. Below, you will find more detailed information about the museums, theatres, art galleries you should visit in the section Art in Albania.

For dining, Tirana offers both a rich traditional cuisine and a variety of foreign fares, from Italian to Chinese, or even Indian. There are also several restaurants on Mount Dajti to discover and enjoy. The mountain is reachable by cable car, which provides a fantastic view of the city. In the Tirana region you may also visit the castles of Petrela and Preza, as well as some natural attractions, such as Pëllumbas Cave, Shkalla e Tujanit, and more. It has an edge, there are lots of things to see and most importantly for any traveller, the alcohol is cheap. Don't forget to visit the raki bar, Komiteti. You can try all the different flavors of raki here and it's set in a sort of museum! It's a cool place to hang out.

Beyond what Tirana has to offer to its visitors, the hospitality shown towards tourists is something that will mark your journey not only in Tirana but also all over the country.

BERAT

BERAT - ALSO KNOWN AS THE TOWN OF ONE THOUSAND windows due to the Ottoman style houses located one near another that Berat is famous for. It is now a UNESCO site as there are over 2000 years of history to explore. The city's life began in the 6th-5th century B.C. as an Illyrian settlement. Later on, it was turned into a castle city known as Antipatrea, which was e expanded afterwards. Inside the castle, they built churches with valuable frescoes and icons, and also a calligraphy school. Uniquely today, residents still live inside of the castle walls. The three major neighborhoods of the old city are Mangalemi, Gorica, and Kala, where the castle itself is located.

When visiting Berat make sure to visit and walk to the top of the castle you to get amazing views of the city of Berat. Within the castle walls, you will also see everyday homes that people still occupy today.

At the foot of the castle you will find an astonishing ensemble of the Byzantine. Some of those extraordinary Byzantine Churches are the Church of Shën Mëhilli (Saint

Michael), while the 13th century Church of Shën Maria e Vllahernës (Saint Mary Blachernae), the Church of Shën Triadha (The Holy Trinity), the post-Byzantine monumental Cathedral of Shën Maria (Saint Mary). This Cathedral houses a museum of works by the famous iconographers of the 16th century: Onufri, and his son, Nikolla. There are over 100 icons on display and they also include works of other artists such as Joan Çetiri, Onufër Qiprioti, and many anonymous painters.

In Mangalemi, below the castle, you can see the famous view of the facades of the houses, with windows that seem to stand above each other. In general, the traditional houses have two floors, where the second floors are noticeable and have many cambered windows and wood carvings. With its houses built along the steep hill, the view of Mangalemi is the reason that another name for Berat is the City of the 1000 Windows or the City of Floating Windows.

Across the Osumi River lies the Gorica neighborhood, whose houses face those of Mangalemi. The arched bridge of Gorica, built in 1780, is a beautiful architectural monument constructed to link Gorica with Mangalemi.

You also can visit the Monastery of Shën Spiridhoni (Saint Spyridon) in Gorica. In 1417, the Ottomans occupied Berat and this conquest left its mark with the building of monuments to the Islamic faith, such as the Xhamia e Kuqe (Red Mosque) inside the castle, the Xhamia e Plumbit (1555), the Xhamia e Beqarëve (Celibataires Mosque) (1872) in Mangalem quartier but also Xhamia Mbret (King Mosque) (16th century), and the Halveti Tekke or Tariqa in the medieval center.

Other sites worth visiting are the Ethnographic Museum, situated inside an 18th century çardak building, and the

Edward Lear Gallery of Art, a well-known English painter who painted much of Berat and Albania.

Besides, if you love outdoor activities and have some time it is suggested to visit the beautiful Tomorr Mountain. If you are a backpacker then make sure you stay at Berat backpackers, it is a great hostel located in one of the most beautiful places in Albania.

In addition Berat is known for its traditional dishes. It is worth tasting specialties such as *pula me përshesh* and *çorba e Tomorrit* in one of the local restaurants. There are also few wineries such as Cabo, Nurellari, Malinati, Luani, where you can taste some great local wines.

GJIROKASTRA

ANOTHER UNESCO SITE WORTH VISITING IS THE GORGEOUS stone city of Gjirokastra. Do not get intrigued like most of the tourist, to either visit Berat or Gjirokastra thinking they may be the same as they both are UNESCO sites. Instead make sure you visit both of them, you will not be disappointed! In Gjirokastra you can visit interesting sites, part of the cultural heritage as well as natural wonders. Cobbled streets, houses made of stone and a castle located at the top, Gijrokastër is worth the visit.

One of the main characteristics of Gjirokastra is the intensive use of stone in building the houses, which look like small fortresses, the streets of cobblestone, which all lead to Bazaar. Due to all these features, Gjirokastra is also known as the "The Stone City".

The origin of the city starts with the castle of Gjirokastra, built in IV century AD. The city was named Argyrokastro, in 1336. In 1417, it was conquered by the Ottoman army. The most important structure of the city is this castle, which is the biggest castle in Albania. There is so much to see inside the castle including underground tunnels, a weapon museum and the abandoned rooms of the castle. Inside you can visit the Museum of Weapons which was opened in 1971. Weapons from the prehistoric times up to the World War II are exhibited on here and you can actually pick up the weapons. Also, the National Folk Festival has taken place in this castle during the years. Make sure you save a few hours for the castle where you can see and climb if you wish on the old army tanks, plus you get amazing views.

During your stay in Gjirokastra, you can visit the Ethnographic Museum, located in the house where the former communist dictator Enver Hoxha was born. This house (today a museum) is located in the Palorto quarter. You can also visit the house of Zekati family in Palorto, in a dominating position, which has undergone restoration. It is one of the most magnificent and characteristic buildings of Gjirokastra. Built in 1811-1812, it is a magnificent three-floor building and has two twin towers. A special feature of the house is the wooden carved ceilings and the characteristic guest room. From the wooden balcony in the third floor, you can enjoy an impressive view of Gjirokastra. Other important traditional buildings to visit are Angonati House, Babaramo newly restored house, Skendulaj house, Eqrem Cabej House under restoration, Kikino House and many others but also the statue of the main square dedicated to the national hero Cerciz Topulli and other important religious monuments of Bektashi sect and Orthodox religion.

Spend an afternoon wandering the streets and people watching from a café. Gijrokastër has a lot of character. One of the famous spots to visit at the Sokaku i te Marreve that means Mad People's Street is also the reconstructed house of the famous Albanian writer Ismail Kadare

The town of Gjirokastra is also known for its culinary art; we can mention special dishes like pasha qofte, shapkat, oshaf with dried figs (a dessert with sheep`s milk, sugar and dried figs), etc.

ANTIGONEA AND HADRIANAPOLIS

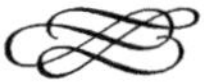

Antigonea

The archaeological park of Antigone is located near Saraqinishte village in the region of Lunxhëria, east of Gjirokastra and only 14km away from it. Antigone was founded by King Pyrrhus of Epirus in 295 B.C., who named the town after his first wife, Antigone. At the end of 3rd century and the beginning of 2nd century BC, it grew into an important economic, cultural and political center and took the form of a state (polis).

It was surrounded by walls, 4,000 meters long. There are many attractions to be visited in the archaeological park Antigone such as: the mosaic, columns, promenade, an antique scale, the surrounding walls, etc. In the village of Labove e Kryqit, located near the small town of Libohova, you can visit one of the oldest and the most beautiful Byzantine churches in Albania, dedicated to St. Mary. It is built in a style similar to that of Hagia Sophia in Istanbul. It was thought that the church used to have a relic, which is missing now. It was part of the cross where Christ was crucified.

Hadrianapolis

The ancient theatre of Hadrianapolis is located near the village of Sofratika, 14 km away from Gjirokastra, along the Gjirokastra - Kakavije (Greece) highway. The Hadrianopolis amphitheater was discovered by the Austrian archaeologist Prashniker. It dates back to the 2nd century B.C; it has a capacity of 4,000 seats and has 27 steps. Cajupi's field lies in Lunxheria area, which is 1,310 meters above sea level; it is a flat area, which is used as climatic resort and surrounded by many sources of cold water.

KRUJA

Kruja is a must-see when you come to Albania. It's only a 45-minute bus ride from Tirana and costs 100 lek. It's well worth staying here if you have the time. Kruja is a small town positioned on the top of a mountain and it is referred to as the city of Skanderbeg. The name and the importance of the city are closely related to the 25 years of activity of the national Albanian hero, Skanderbeg. He fought and rallied the troops against the Ottoman Empire and saved the Albanians from being taken over by the Ottomans. In the fifteenth century he made the city of Kruja a bastion of uncompromising resistance against the Ottoman Empire.

The Gjergj Kastrioti Skanderbeg Museum is situated inside the castle walls, which date back to the fifth and sixth centuries A.D. The museum itself was inaugurated in 1981. Within the walls of the castle are also the Ethnographic Museum and the Dollma Tekke. If you are interested in Albanian history, the castle and these museums are remarkable for learning more about.

Near the castle's entrance is a traditional market, which dates back to the period of Skanderbeg. There are also the most incredible markets which are hundreds of years old. Here tourists will find little treasures from the most beautiful antiques, unique Albanian souvenirs, such as craft products, embroidered items, carpeting, silver objects, copper, alabaster, filigree, traditional clothing, antiques at the traditional Old Baazar of Kruja.

If you end up staying in Kruja, stay in one of the original houses within the castle walls, the Emiliano rooms. It is affordable and beautiful. Also, make sure to have a traditional Albanian dinner while there.

SHKODRA

SHKODRA IS LOCATED IN THE NORTHERN PART OF ALBANIA near the lake Skutari at the boarder to Montenegro. It is a very picturesque city very rich in cultural heritage. The architecture is unlike anywhere else in Albania. You may notice that you have stepped back in time into an old-fashioned film, that's the charm of Shkodra. It is really artistic city with really strong traditions and culture. Shkodra is one of the most important cities of Albania and is also known to be the center of Albanian Catholicism, Culture and Harmony between different religions. Also, it is widely known as the cradle of culture in Albania. The city itself, as well as the people bears pride in the large number of artists, musicians, painters, photographers, poets, and writers born here.

In Shkoder, you will notice that the culture and the language of the people are different from the other parts of the country. The culture and the speaking dialect of cities in the northern and the southern part of Albania is quite different. The northern part of Albania, including Shkodra speaks the *gege* dialect, while the southern part of the country speaks the *toske* dialect, which is closer to the official Albanian language. Another interesting thing that you will notice in Shkoder, is the biking culture of the locals. Shkodra is the city of bikes, everyone's biking!

One of the main tourist attractions is the Rozafa Castle. Rising majestically upon a rocky hill west of the city, the outcroppings and battlements paint a blazing picture against the setting sun. The castle is surrounded by the waters of three rivers; the Drini, Buna, and Kiri. As the town itself, the castle has Illyrian origins too and it is known as one of the strongest areas of the Labeats (Illyrian tribe).

As most of the ancient sites, this castle has an enchanting and a heart-wrenching popular legend. Rozafa was the name of the wife of the youngest of three brothers who originally built the castle. The three men worked tirelessly by day laying mortar and stone to build the walls, yet every night thy crumbled. The tree brothers decided to consult a wise man, who said that in order to expel the evil attacking at their daily work and protect their friends and family with a strong castle that would last through the ages, one of their wives needed to be entombed within the walls. The brothers made a pact that they should not tell their wives about this danger, and whose wife brought her husband his noon meal she is the one who will be sacrificed the following day. The younger brother kept his word, while the elder brothers broke their word and told their wives. So, and it was Rozafa alone who came with food. When she heard the proclamation, she wept for her newborn son and husband, but allowed herself to become a living part of the walls so that the castle could be built. According to both legend and local folklore, the water flowing at the entrance of the castle is the milk flowing from one of her breasts, which she requested be left exposed so that she could feed her baby. She also pleaded for one foot and one arm to be left free, in order to rock her son's cradle at night and sooth him during the day. This beautiful and heart broking legend is one of the reasons why this castle is widely known!

On the other hand, a more scientific of the castle's history is given by the historians who claim that the castle reflects the dominion of the Balshaj family but passed through enough other ruling periods that each left their own signs and markings on the grounds, including a distinct Venetian flare, some Ottoman architecture from the 16th and 17th centuries. Moreover, within the castle walls is a museum where if you are a lover of antiquities, you can spend a comfortable afternoon reading and learning more about its history, as well as tasting the delicious local food in the restaurant within.

During your stay, you can also visit the renewed Marubi National Museum of Photography famous for its big and rare collection of photos over Albanian history. You can also just take a tour in the old center of the city; pass through churches or mosques, at Pedonalja also known as Kole Idromeno. The Theatre Migjeni will offer you a chance to see and admire concerts or performances depending on the season you are visiting.

Another suggested activity in Shkodra, is visiting its lake. You can bath or you can just enjoy the nature while having your lunch or dinner. If you happen to visit this lake do not miss one of the most delicious dishes of the region – *Krap ne tave* (carp).

Sure you will find plenty of things to do and experience in Shkodra, for incredibly affordable prices!

ANCIENT CITY OF APOLLONIA

THE REMINISCENT RUIN OF THE ANCIENT GREEK AND ILLYIRAN city, Apollonia, is located in the southwestern Albania, about 13 miles from the city of Fier near the village of Pojan. It is one of the most well - known archeological sites in the country and a UNESCO world heritage site full of history.

According to the tradition it was founded during the first half of the 6th century BC by Corinth, a Greek colonist from Corfu, led by Gylax, which named the city after his name - Gylakeia. Right after its foundation the city changed its name to Apollonia, named after the powerful divinity Apollo. It stands on a sit on a windswept hilltop from where expands the fertile plain of Musacchia with the Adriatic Sea and the hills of Mallakastra. Quickly after its foundation this city became one of the most eminent cities of the Adriatic basin, which was mentioned more frequently from the other 30 (thirty) cities bearing the same name during Antiquity. The city lay in the territory of the political communion of the Taulantii and was broadly known as Apollonia of Illyria. The culture and the general development of the city maintained a clear Greek character throughout its existence. However, the independent economic and politic activity as well as the close relationships with the Illyrian hinterland determined a distinctive physiognomy of the apollonian culture.

The ruins of Apollonia were discovered in the beginning of the 19th century. It is said, that nowadays only 5% of Apollonia has been discovered, as a large part of the ruins remain buried under the ground. This is truly incredible because as you walk around the park you will soon understand how much is yet to still be discovered.

The fascinating landscape of the archeological park, which has been preserved in an exceptionally intact condition, comprises a successful combination between the beauty of monuments and nature, attractive through its long history, in an atmosphere of relaxation and meditation. The ruins are still impressing and show a little piece of the original glory. The historical place is very impressing. The view from the hills to the country is worth it as well.

Libraries, temples, theatres and other buildings can be visited, as well as a triumphal arch and rotted mansions. This archaeological park or site contains also a Museum of Archaeology that is situated at the old Monastery of Saint Mary.

BUTRINT ARCHEOLOGICAL PARK

BUTRINT IS ONE OF THE MAIN HISTORICAL SITES OF COUNTRY, A – a UNESCO protected area. Butrint was inhabited in the 6th century BC by the Greeks and later the Romans took over. But, Butrint was inhabited well before that, in the prehistoric times. Archaeological research shows that the earliest evidence of life dates back to 50,000 years ago.

This is one of the sites worth visiting, not just for its unrivaled beauty and historical importance, but also since it is located in one of the most beautiful coastal areas, nearby Saranda and behind the Ksamil beach. It is surrounded by nature and the Vivari channel. April is the best time to visit this park when the weather is good, nature is in bloom, and tourist crowds are few and especially early in the morning.

The ruins, which are in a fantastic natural setting and are part of a 29-sq-km national park, are from a variety of periods, spanning 2500 years. The park is incredibly big; you can easily spend the whole day here exploring all that it has to offer. There's one restaurant within the park at the top otherwise there's also another one down the road. I highly recommend looking at Ali Pasha fortress which is not too far from the main park at Butrint. You can reach it by catching a ride with a local fisherman or walking down from the viewpoint on the road going towards Butrint.

VLORE

LOCATED ON THE SOUTHEASTERN ADRIATIC SEA, IT IS THE beginning or the end of the Albanian Riviera and is Vlora is the second biggest harbor of the country. Also, it is one of the most frequented areas and important points for Albanian tourism offering both "sea and sun". Vlore is a coastal city, much bigger than the other cities such as Saranda. It also is a really old city was founded in the 6th century BC and firstly it used to be named Aulona.

This beautiful city is not only known for the beautiful and the crystal clear beaches, but, it carries a special historical importance for Albanians. Vlore is the city which hosted the First National Assembly, which declared the country's independence from Ottoman Empire on November 28th, 1912. The Museum of Independence is dedicated to this historic event. Other museums include the ethnographic and historic ones.

You have lots of things to do and see around Vlore. Highly recommended is the Muradije Mosque, the only work remaining in Albania from the famous architect Sinan the

Great, built in 1542. On the top of the hill overlooking the city is the religious point of Kuzum Baba. Located in this region are the Orikum and Amantia archaeological parks, and the Llogara National Park.

Also, I would suggest going to the castle, you get spectacular views of the city from here. Sazan Island is also close and is the largest island in Albania. It's a military zone but recently it started opening in the summer for tourists to come see

There are plenty of beaches in Vlore to check out too. The beach area near the city is well known for its new and modern hotels along with other facilities like bars, restaurants, clubs, and cafes. This is one of the most exciting tourist areas of the country. That area starts directly south of the city along the small and rocky beaches of the Bay of Vlorë. Further down the harbor of Orikum you will find a recently built yacht harbor.

POGRADEC

RIGHT ON THE BORDER OF MACEDONIA IS A POPULAR STOPOVER holiday spot for families. This town is a must for nature lovers who are after a peaceful holiday by the lake. Pogradec offers beautiful views of Lake Ohrid which is over 4 million years old. The lake is under UNESCO protection as it is home to as many as 17 aquatic animal species which are majority native to this lake.

The road to the region of Pogradec is the national highway where the road from Macedonia crosses Qafë Thanë and passes along the shore of the Lake Ohrid. This crossroad offers picturesque views of the Lake Ohrid, a true pearl nestled between Mali i Thatë (the Dry Mountain) to the east and the Mokra highland to the west. This lake is divided by the Albanian – Macedonian border, one part is in Ohrid and the other in Pogradec (hereinafter Pogradeci lake).

This tectonic lake is considered to be two to four million years old, and is the deepest of its kind in the Balkans, reaching a maximum depth of 285 meters. The lake environment is a natural habitat for a variety of old flora and fauna. It is under UNESCO protection due to its unique value and is home 17 species of aquatic animals, 70% of which are native and 30% migrant. The sponge of this lake is found only here and in Lake Baikal. It houses the rare fish "Koran," a kind of trout, impossible to find in almost any other lake in the world.

By the shore of the lake you will find a vast array of restaurants, clubs, and comfortable hotels. You must not miss a taste of the traditional fish dishes, especially the rare fish Koran specialty Tave Korani (baked speckled trout), as well as the famous pickles. You might also sample the various wines on offer, but don't miss the traditional unique wine of Buti, or the famous Perla and Moskat raki of Pogradec.

The city, with its mild climate, lends itself to year-round visits. Before leaving Pogradec don't miss Drilon and Tushemisht, just 4-5 km south of the city. The Drilon waters form a small lake, surrounded by beautiful greenery that makes the area and the nearby village of Tushemisht a unique oasis of beauty and tranquility. Don't forget about the wonderful restaurants in the area, constructed from wood and offering some of the most delicious dishes of the region.

A little further down, just about 25 km outside of Pogradec, you might stop at the Lin peninsula and in the village of the same name to admire the enchanting views. Mosaics of Lin, date back to the 7th-6th BC and it is said that in ancient times, this was the favorite holiday destination of the Roman Emperor Justinian's parents. This ancient artwork exhibits an amazing ensemble of zoomorphic, floral, and geometric decorations.

The region of Pogradec is rich in striking and distinctive

natural and historical monuments. You might visit the natural monument, the Rock of Kamje, which is located in the commune of Dardhas (on the way from Pogradec to Korça, near the village of Osnat). It is 70 m high and suddenly rises out of the surrounding terrain like a "ship sailing in a sea of green." The Church of Marena, The archaeological site and Monumental Graves of Selca lie 30 km away from Pogradec. The monuments here date back to the 4th century B.C. and the five monumental stone graves are found in very few places elsewhere in the Balkans.

KORÇA

Korça is a city located near the Albanian-Macedonian and Greek border and is set in a valley so the city is surrounding by mountains. Korca is one of the most important and charming ski destinations in Albania. The locals usually tend to spend their winter holidays in this beautiful region where there are plenty of opportunities for outdoor activities. In Korçë you can do skiing, ice skating and hiking in the breathtaking mountains of the surrounding area and enjoy gorgeous winter scenery.

Korca is a historical city with a lovely café culture. So after a cold day in the nearby mountains, go for a visit to the city center, relax, get a hot drink and warm up in of the cafés at *Pazari i Vjeter* (the old market). When you come to Albania you will no doubt try one of the local beers Korça. Well, you can visit the city when Korça is made and produced. The best thing about it is that you will get beer for the wholesale price. That means you will pay a pittance for a bottle of beer, that's insane! During the winter season, if you don't want to spend your holiday in urban areas and instead you

FINIQ

FINIQ IS A HIDDEN GEM, LOCATED JUST OUT OF SARANDA. IT IS incredibly under-visited and unexplored site that most of the tourists are not even aware of its existence, which is a vast loss. The Finiq archaeological park is still mostly yet to be discovered but there's a Roman theatre, Hellenistic houses, a small temple, Byzantine church and lots of relics. The site was formed in the second half of the 5th century BC.

From the park, you gain amazing views of the surrounding landscape. It's a very peaceful place. I highly recommend taking a picnic up to the site and enjoying the view and history!

ALBANIAN COASTLINE AND BEACHES

THE REPUBLIC OF ALBANIA HAS A CONSIDERABLE COASTLINE that stretches for 450 km (including lagoons) and extends along the Adriatic and the Ionian Sea. It is easy to tell the seas apart thanks to their different characteristics.

In this section we will have a look at the most outstanding beaches and places all over the Albanian coastline, firstly, starting from the very top, i.e. the Adriatic Coast.

THE ADRIATIC COAST

The beaches of the Adriatic are generally sandy and have shallow waters, making them perfect for family holidays. Among other beaches, the main ones are those of Velipoja, Shëngjin, Durrës, Golem, Spillenja, Divjaka. Besides the beaches, the Adriatic coast is rich in lagoons and other natural ecosystems providing wonderful opportunities for those passionate about the study and observation of birds or eco - tourism. If you want to spend a day in birds' prey, pack the binoculars and go straight to the coastal wetlands of

Karavasta for bird watch. Part of the Divjake-Karavasta National Park, the lagoon is the westernmost breeding site of the Dalmatian Pelican. For further bird watching, visit Kune – Vaini – natural reserve, nearby the Drini River. This reserve is found just south of the town of Shengjin, and this area is well known for its natural beauty and wildlife, and also marked to be home to many birds such as eagles, spoonbills and herons.

Velipoja beach

It is the northernmost beach of the country situated 22 km away from city of Shkodra. Close by, is the lagoon of Viluni and the alluvial island of Franc Joseph, located in the proximity of the mouth of Buna, all representing particularly attractive ecosystem for those interested in ecotourism and nature lovers in general. The beach, with 4 km of high quality sand, is suitable for family vacations and is generally visited by northern Albanians, tourists from Kosovo and Montenegro. Velipoja is a famous beach in Albania known for the quality of its curative sand.

The temperature is just lovely, beginning from the mid-May it is usually above 20°C, and it is blessed with around 250 sunny days. If you choose to spend few days of your vacation in Velipoja, it means you are doing a great healthy gift to yourself, because of the curative sand, fresh air and green area that surrounds its shore.

Shëngjin beach

Shengjin is a growing beach town located in Northwest Albania, near the district of Lezha, situated 8 km away from the historic town of Lezha. Shëngjin beach as well is well - known for its high quality sand and has 200-300 sunny days per year. Just along the north part of Shëngjin, ahead of Renci hills, lays the wonderful beach called Rana e Hedhun (the Thrown Sand), which is well protected from the winds of that area. Rana e Hedhun is an undeveloped stretch of coastline well known for its sand dunes and seascape near the mountain ridge. Shengjin is quickly becoming one of the must see locations in Albania for day trippers or those looking for a relaxing getaway by the coast.

Gjiri i Lalezit (Bay of Lalzi Beach)

Gjiri i Lalezit is another attractive area of the Adriatic coastline, located at around 30 km north of Durrës, hiding behind beautiful tall trees and the songs of the cicadas, and it is perhaps the most popular and populated beach along the long Adriatic coast. The beaches of Lalëzi Bay are sandy, some surrounded by strips of pine trees. It offers spectacular views of the tree-lined cliffs as well as the beautiful scenery of the Adriatic Sea. Its many recreational facilities keep the people busy playing beach volley and all kinds of other sports. In the hot summer months, in particular, the bars and restaurants are crowded.

This beautiful destination is situated between Rodon and Bishti i Pallës Cape. Rodon Cape is another wonderful beach nearby, a natural masterpiece of 7.5 km length and it is a huge draw for those who enjoy diving. This narrow strip of land, in the shape of a peninsula, extends along the Adriatic and offers not only beautiful views but several crucial historical and cultural monuments. Many tourists choose to visit the Cape of Rodon during the spring season as it is shrouded in a beautiful cornucopia of flowers, while in the summer, they choose it to enjoy the beautiful virgin beaches and fine-grained sand.

Durrës Beach

Another striking beach along the Adriatic coastline is the Durres beach. This beach is the closest one to the capital city of Tirana, situated only 39 km away. The buzzing atmosphere of this major seaside town, and its close vicinity to the capital, make the beautiful beaches of this seaside town the most popular and visited weekend destinations, year-round. The locals from the nearby cities, especially from Tirana even head towards this destination even just for daily visits, to spend a lovely beach day.

Durres is the biggest beach and has a length of 6 km with a considerably wide strip of sand. The sea depth increases very gradually, which makes this beach very safe for families and kids. In Durres, there are three major beaches:

North of Durrës, the beach of Currila or Kallm beach is deeper and is quite protected by warm wind coming from the land.

South of Durrës you will find two other beaches: Golem and Mali i Robit, with characteristics similar to the beaches around the Durrës area.

The beaches of Durrës are especially nostalgic for the local population as they were historically the most frequented by families and, while the nostalgic air still lingers, the town has become a veritable modern international touristic attraction. With lots to do and only one hour away from Tirana, you will enjoy your time there.

. . .

THE ALBANIAN RIVIERA

The Albanian Riviera perhaps is the most popular place in the country for tourists to visit along with the capital city, Tirana. The reason is that it is just amazing: long sandy and pebble beaches lapped by turquoise water, and lovely coastal hamlets with small Orthodox churches, cobblestoned streets and flowers everywhere. The Albanian Riviera is blessed with 300 days of sun. The average temperature in January is 10 degrees C. and the average temperature in July is 25 degrees C.

The Albanian Riviera also generally known as *Bregu,* should not be confused with the entire Albanian coastline. This is the coastline along the Northeastern Ionian Sea in the Mediterranean Sea, encompassing the districts of Sarandë and Vlorë in Southwestern Albania. It forms an important section of the Albanian Ionian Sea Coast dotted with the villages of Palasë, Dhërmi, Vuno, Himara, Qeparo, Borsh, Piqeras and Lukovë.

The Albanian Riviera is known for having fascinating beaches with deep and very clean waters. Some of the most exotic and interesting beaches in the south of Albania are Dhërmi, Jale, Himara, Qeparo, Borsh, Saranda and Ksamil. From the Llogara Pass, which is 1,057 meters above sea level, the breathtaking coast can be seen as if from the vantage point of an airplane. The seaside town of Himara is one of the Riviera's best places to visit, while Porto Palermo Beach, Llamani Beach and Filikuri Beach are some of the area's finest sandy stretches, while Drymades Beach is one of the liveliest spots here.

Younger crowds tend to visit the Ionian beaches as the area offers many opportunities for those interested in water sports like diving, boat tours, etc. Also, the area is a major nightlife, ecotourism, and elite retreat destination in Albania. It features traditional Mediterranean villages, ancient castles, churches, monasteries, secluded turquoise beaches, bays, mountain passes, seaside canyons, coves, rivers, underwater fauna, caves, and orange, lemon, and olive groves. The Riviera has a growing reputation as an important music location, with many international music festivals – including Turtle Fest and Sound wave Albania – having taken place here. Nightclubs such as Folie Marine in Jale beach and Havana Beach Club near Dhermi draw young people from across Europe to the Albanian Riviera.

THE IONIAN COAST

Dhraleos – Palasë

The first beach in the Ionian Coast of the Albanian Riviera is Dhraleos in Palasë. It has a length of 1.5 km and is one of the most exotic and serene beaches of the Albanian coastal zone complete with rich blue clean waters. This beach is popular for water sports and is sometimes even the destination for the parachutes that launch from Llogara Pass.

Dhermi

Dhërmi is located a little further south and is becoming one of the most frequented and important tourist places along the Albanian Riviera and the Albanian coast entirely.

Dhermi is a great place to spend your summer vacation as it is in the middle of some other great places and beaches to visit in Albania. The crystal-clear waters, isolated beaches, water sports and diving make this the preferred beach of younger generation. Dhermi has some great beaches and the town is made for tourists, lots of accommodation and restaurant options here. You can choose to stay right on the beach or in the village above.

The different beaches that are part of Dhërmi are Jaliksari, Shkambo and Gjipea. Make sure if you stay in Dhermi to make a trip to Gjipe beach. It's one of the best beaches in Albania - a hidden gem in between a canyon. Throughout this entire area, family tourism has developed, where tourists can choose to rent guesthouses or reside in a variety of hotels nearby.

Vuno

Only 8 km south of Dhërmi, you will find the village of Vuno, which is the central area of the Albanian Riviera. Vuno is one of the northernmost sea-facing villages in Himara Province, and is often named as "the mountain ridge acropolis". Cut by the national road, above it the village disperses on the hillside, with pathways and arched passages linking the stacks of houses, while below, it expands and entwines with the cascading landscape seeming to join the seaside below. Here the architecture is unique, more noticeably the Tower of Shane Koka, and the dwelling of Odise Kasneci with traditional stone and woodwork.

Vuno is one of those hidden gems that usually remains off the tourist radar and often missed. It is a very small village along the Albanian Riviera trail. Stone houses and cobbled stone paths lead throughout the village. You gain magnificent views over the olive groves and the beaches of the Albanian Riviera.

This charming little village was abandoned but today it is slowly being revived. This little tourist village comes to life during the summer season due to the younger generations that go to enjoy the beautiful beach or the Outdoor Festival of Vuno.

Gjipe Beach

Gjipe beach is not too far away from Vuno, and it is a great thing to go see if you end up visiting Vuno for a night or two. The beach of Gjipea has a beautiful shape. Past this beach there is a stream that has made a canyon with 70 meters high walls. Located near the beach of Dhërmi is the Cave of Pirates which tourists can access only by boat or ferry. There are also hotels, restaurants and summer clubs located nearby.

Jale

Jale is a beach town which has become popular in recent years. This is a great option for a beach vacation and there are many accommodation options, including campsites, beach parties and the perfect place to relax. You can hire a kayak and visit some of the nearby hidden coves and beaches, Gjipe beach being one of them.

Himara Beach

Himara is a small sunny town located in southern Albania. It is a less busy beach town located a few hours' drive north of Saranda with a great potential for development of the tourism. The population amounts around 28,000 people including and some of the above-mentioned villages and not only. It is characterized by its seaside promenade with some really good restaurants *tavernas* and the traditionally preserved old town built on a hill, which you should definitely check out. Himare has a more relaxed, chilled vibe than the likes of Saranda. The views are incredibly pretty and it is the perfect place if you want to chill out by the beach for a few days.

The town of Himarë consists of the old town, Kastro, situated on and around the old castle and the coastal region of Spilea, which is the touristic and economic center of the region. Other parts of the town are Potami, Livadhi, Zhamari, Michaili and Stefaneli. North of the town of Himarë lie the villages of Vuno, Ilias, Dhërmi, with its coastal region Jaliskari, and Palasë. Dhermi contains a number of recently built beach resorts. On the mountains lie Pilur and Kudhës, while Qeparo lies to the south of the town of Himarë.

I highly recommend making a trip to the old part of Himare which is in the hills, next to the castle. From there you get incredible views of the Riveria and you also get to see a traditional village, which is so pretty.

The region has several Orthodox churches and monasteries, built in the traditional Byzantine architecture, like the Monastery of the Cross, Athaliotissa, Saint Theodore, Virgin Mary in Dhërmi and Saint Demetrius. Moreover, a number of churches are located inside the castle of Himarë, which was initially built in classical antiquity, like the Church of Virgin Mary, Episkopi, which is built on the site of an ancient temple dedicated to Apollo, as well as the Aghioi Pantes church, in the entrance of the castle.

. . .

Borsh

Another great place to visit along the Albanian Riviera is Borsh. Borsh is also very chilled and holds the longest stretch of beach in Albania. It's situated in between olive groves and is a nice place to get away from the craziness of Saranda in the summer. Borsh, is one of the longer beach areas of the Albanian Riviera protected by a collection of massive Mediterranean vegetation, primarily citrus and olive plantations. Family tourism has also become very popular in this area. Between here and the city of Saranda, one can find the beaches of Bunec, Kakome and Krokëy whose collective length runs about three km and each with beautiful, crystal-clear water.

I highly recommend making a trip to Borsh castle which sits on the mountain overlooking the beach. The castle is in ruins, but it's often missed by tourists and is completely forgotten. The views are stunning. There's also an old mosque in the castle walls which was added by the Ottomans. It's not a working mosque as it is nearly completely ruined but its beautiful inside and you can still see some of the paintings on the ceiling.

Qeparo

There are two parts to Qeparo – the old and the new or the upper side and the downside. You definitely should not miss this village. The Upper Qeparo is magical. It is the perfect place to see a traditional Albanian village, but there is a twist. This part of the Qeparo is half abandoned. After the fall of communist system many of the villagers left this place and immigrated to other countries leaving the village completely abandoned. These days about half of the village has been renovated but many of the old stone houses remain still neglected and ruined. The streets are cobbled, the views are magnificent, and history is rich here. There is not much to do apart from admire and gaze at this beautiful village. Lower Qeparo is situated right on the beach and is a chilled out little beach town.

After Borsh and Qeparo, there is the small tectonic gulf of Porto Palermo where Ali Pasha castle is located.

Porto Palermo

The Porto Palermo castle and its beach are a great stopover during a holiday to the Albanian Riviera. The castle was built in the 19th century and belonged to Ali Pasha. The castle is unique because it is in a star shape instead of the usual 4 corners a castle normally has.

You will also see old army barracks beside the castle and nearby there's also a submarine bunker. Despite the fact that the beach is small and rocky, it is still a lovely place to stop by. There are also, many backpackers camping on the beach and the nearby area.

Saranda

The city of Saranda is the most populous urban area on the Albanian Riviera and during the summer it is one of the most popular tourist destinations in Albania. The city is well-located on the coast only 9 km away from the Greek island of Corfu. Daily ferries offer connections between Saranda and Corfu making this southern Albanian city a good base for European and international tourists. Saranda is well connected with cruisers that come from all over the world and Corfu, during summer is mostly full of tourists from all over Europe.

What was once a sleepy fishing village is now a thriving town, and while Saranda had lost much of its charm; however, in the past two decades it has rapidly revived. The town's name comes from Ayii Saranda, an early monastery dedicated to 40 saints; its bombed remains are still high on the hill above the town.

Saranda is a charming beach town in Albanian Riviera and a great mix of beach life, good restaurants and the main location in Albania for nightlife. During the summer a substantial number of Albanians come here to live and work for the high tourist season so the nightlife here is very prominent. During the summer it is really crowded, and feels like half of Albanians head towards Saranda to enjoy the busy beach and busier nightlife along its crowd-filled seaside promenade. When the winter starts it turns into a sleepy beach town but still boasts great weather as Saranda is blessed with over 300 days of sunshine a year. The city and surrounding areas offer a range of accommodation; from hotels catering to five-star travelers as well as the more budget conscious, while home rentals also remain an option.

Saranda is a great base for exploring the beaches around such as Pulebardhat , Pasqyrat , Manastiri beaches ect., or going to Ksamil beaches and Butrint Unesco World Heritage Site if you have your own transport or also take a taxi or use the public transport . You can also visit the small castle of Lekursi that offer a spectacular view and a good restaurant or the monastery of Saint George very well conserved and restored.

Along Saranda you will find some smaller beaches like Central and Liman. Usually, the most preferred tourist destination is Ksamil, which is located in the Ksamil Peninsula and is a part of the Butrint National Park hosting a number of hotels and restaurants, near the beach of Ksamil. It also has few small islands covered by Mediterranean vegetation

Ksamil

One of the breathtaking places in Albania that will leave you speechless is Ksamil. It is a village and a former municipality in the Riviera of Southern Albania, and part of Butrint National Park. At the 2015 local government reform it became a subdivision of the municipality Sarandë. Located in the southern of the city of Sarandë off the road to Butrint, only a 20-minute bus ride from Saranda is this beautiful paradise.

Ksamil Beach and Albania's Ionian Coast further north was included in The Guardian's 20 of the best bargain beach holidays for 2013. It is one of the most frequented coastal resorts by both domestic and foreign tourists. Ksamil is often referred to as the most beautiful place in Albania and for good reason, it is indeed stunning. The sand is white, the beach is small but its water is crystal clear. One of main attractions are the nearby Ksamil Islands which you can swim out to as well as you can rent a jet ski or paddle boat and spend the day relaxing in the Albanian sun.

It is more preferable to visit Ksamil in any other time except the high tourist season in July and August. During those two months, the place is extremely crowded full with tourists. It's much more enjoyable to visit during one of the shoulder season when most of the summer tourists have left and there are only a few sunbeds left.

NATURE & OUTDOORS

BESIDES THE THRILLING AND LIVELY CITIES IN ALBANIA, there's also a wealth of natural destinations in this relatively undiscovered country in the Western Balkans.

Albania is abundantly mountainous country, about two-thirds of the territory either hilly or mountainous. Therefore, the national parks claim and deserve, the spotlight.

Albania's National Parks spread from the lagoons at the Adriatic coastline to the Limestone Mountains of the Dinaric Alps and the wetlands of the Great and the Small Prespa Lakes at the trans-border national park, which Albania shares with the Republic of Macedonia and Greece. Some of those Albania national parks are also known beyond the country's borders, attracting adventurers from near and far. Good examples are Llogara, Theth, and Butrint (the UNESCO World Heritage Site). However, there are quite more national parks that still need to be discovered more, like Albania in its entirety.

The highest peak, Mount Korabi, on the border with Macedonia, is about 2,751 m above the sea level. The cliffs of Llogara, dividing the Adriatic from the Ionian Coast, are internationally renowned as one of the best places in the Balkans for paragliding. Undeniably, Albania is very suitable destination for both holidays on the beach, as well as outdoor activities. Getting outdoors is one of the must-do things to do in Albania.

Its undiscovered, veiled beauty will certainly surprise you and make you want to come all over again.

Some of the outdoor activities available in Albania, include hiking, trekking, mountain climbing, mountain biking, wildlife and bird watching, fishing, horseback riding, landscape photography, rock climbing skiing, ski shoeing and winter mountaineering. Rivers crisscross this land and offer both the beauty of the canyons they have carved and the opportunity to traverse them via raft, kayak, or canoe.

Without further ado, let's have a look at the main national parks in Albania, and what you can do there to get the utmost use of its beautiful nature!

The National Parks in Albania

Parks with a diverse terrain, suitable for sightseeing, fishing, relaxation, recreation, mountain climbing and winter sports. They offer opportunities for excursions, skiing, sky sports, mountain climbing, etc.

The National Park of "Mali i Dajtit" (Dajti Mountain)

. . .

This national park is located to the east part of the capital city of Tirana and has an area of 3,300 ha and it is 1,611m above sea level. It is easily accessible from the city, just 25 km to its east. The cable car station is just 20 minutes by car or bus from centre of Tirana, and from where you take the cable car to have a delightful experience. Just after 15 minutes you are near the top of the mountain where there are magnificent panoramic views of the city, villages, forests, the sea, and traditional houses, as well as original peculiarities such as the bunkers.

A typical feature of the Dajti National Park is the change of the types of vegetation with the increase in altitude. Mediterranean shrubs and evergreen makia type vegetation grow 300 – 600 meters above the sea level. Oak trees and shrubs grow at 500 (600) – 1,000 (1,300) meters of altitude – an area which is also characterized by a mix of tree varieties. The Park has also a rich, diverse and well-developed animal life. It is an important habitat for the large mammals, such as wild boar, wolf, badger, fox, wild hare, brown bear, bats, etc.

Dajti Park is also well frequented by daily visitors as well as for the weekend trips. Accommodation for longer stays is available. The Park offers is perfect for relaxation and sightseeing and there are sufficient opportunities for excursions, skiing, sky sports, mountain climbing, etc. If you are visiting Tirana, and want to have a rest from the crowded city, Mount Dajti is one of the best destinations you can have. It is a unspoiled place to relax and breathe in fresh air, taking you far from the buzzing city below. There are many restaurants on the mountain where you can enjoy delicious food or alternatively you can take a picnic with friends and family to the park. The Park is a wonderful place throughout the year, but especially in summer, a place to breathe fresh air, while in winter the mountain and park are covered in snow.

The National Park of "Llogara"

This park is located near the city of Vlora, 40 km to its southeast, on the border between the Adriatic and Ionian seas. The Park is crossed by the national road Vlorë – Himarë – Sarandë as well as by pathways that promote visits by eco tourists.

The altitude increases from 470 meters to 2,018 meters. This Park offers wonderful and captivating landscapes inside, at places of unique character. The Llogara pass is one of the most beautiful drives in Europe. You gain stunning views of the Ionian Sea and a good part of the Albanian Riviera, particularly some of the best beaches located in the the villages of Palasa, Dhërmi, Vuno, etc.

The environment in Llogara is characterized by heterogeneity, manifested in the variety of trees and plants. You might encounter trees of very unique shapes, a result of wind currents.

One such example is the "Flag Pine-Tree", a rare natural monument with scientific and touristic interest. Also, the ecosystem includes numerous habitats that sustain a great number of species, 105 kinds of birds, among which 6 both rare and under danger of extinction. The mammals in the park include the wolf, fox wild cat, deer, marten, badger, an

The Park of Llogara is an important tourist destination, but also a bridge to the Ionian seashore. It is amenable to the promotion of ecotourism, sky sports, excursions, trekking. It is a climacteric location where the mountain air combines with that of the sea. If you love hiking, then good news because Llogara is the gateway for the Karaburun Peninsula. There is still not a lot of information about this peninsula as it's the most untouched part of the Albanian Riviera. To get to the hidden coves and beaches you must hike for 4-6 hours one way and there are no certain tracks yet.

The Park offers accommodation for the enthusiasts of sky sports.

Llogara National Park is great for a summer or winter getaway. Within the park, you have many options – hiking, paragliding, camping and you're also close to the sea!

The National Park "Butrinti"

It is located around 25 km to the south of the town of Saranda. It has a significant importance from the scientific, archeological, touristic, social and recreational perspective. The ancient city of Butrint lies inside one such forest, a true subtropical jungle, dominated by high trees and laurel. This is an area of particular significance for tourism in Albania, primarily the cultural tourism targeting the ancient city of Butrint, protected by the UNESCO, the blue tourism in Ksamil, ecotourism, water sports, fishing in the lake of Butrint, etc.

Its biodiversity is of both national and international significance. The sector Canal of Çuka – inlet and islands of Ksamil is especially appealing and relaxing. The islands are like an oasis of wonderful sights of the sea and land. They are covered by lavish typical Mediterranean vegetation.

The National Park of "Thethi"

Situated in the Albanian Alps, in the proximity of Bjeshkët e Nemuna (Cursed Mountains), Theth is about 70 km away from the city of Shkodra. Located in the north, Theth national park is one, if not the most beautiful national park in Albania. Theth is a picturesque village hidden in the mountains. From here you can start some great hikes through the Albanian Alps. Through the Park runs the beautiful Thethi River, which flows as fast as 1,000 – 1,300 l/sec., and is rich in mountain trout.

Thethi National Park stands out for its diversity of habitats and kinds of vegetation; approximately 1,500 types of plants grow in this Park. They represent almost half of the varieties that exist in the whole country. The fauna of the Thethi Park is diverse too. Among many types of mammals, the Park is known for housing the largest population (50 heads) of bobcats (lynx-lynx) in the country, a species in danger of extinction.

Theth is a haven for lovers of wild animals and beautiful nature. Over 2/3rds of the park is covered in trees. Theth is isolated but the tourism is rapidly developing. There's an abundance of things to see including the park itself, springs, waterfalls, stone carvings and more. One of the most beautiful things to see is the canyon at the ravine of Shkalla e Thethit (Stair of Thethi), an area inhabited by wild doves, is approximately 40 meters high and one meter wide. Also, Grunas cataract is especially picturesque and captivating with water falling from a height of 30 meters.

If you visit the Park you can engage in a number of activities, such as mountain climbing, winter sports, fishing, kayaking, speleological expeditions, mountain biking.

. . .

The National Park "Mali i Tomorrit" (the Mountain of Tomorr),

The Mountain of Tomorr is located to the east of the UNESCO protected city of Berat. It includes the highest peak for the region of Central and Southern Albania, 2,415.7 meters above the sea level and from afar away appears like a gigantic natural citadel. The ruins of the old castle found in the near the Tomorri village affirm the ancient history of this area.

This Park is beautiful in every season of the year. The Park is endowed by a rich flora and fauna. Typical are beech-only forests or those mixed with mountain pine-wood. The most frequently seen animals are the brown bear, wolf, fox, marten, and badger. You can engage in winter sports, mountain climbing, trekking, as well as pilgrimages.

Visitors interested in religious traditions would find this pilgrimage of great interest. You can find the Tyrbe of Kulmak (a place of worship), 1,200 meters above the sea level, which houses the tomb of Abaz Aliu. Every year, at the end of August, thousands of people climb to this location in a week-long ritual of the Bektashi sect.

National Park of "Lura"

This national park is located in the eastern slope of the massif "Kunora e Lurës" (the Crown of Lura). It has an area of 1,280 ha and an altitude of 1,350 – 1,720 meters above the sea level. The 14 glacial lakes which during the winter freeze, offer a most scenic and fascinating sight. Among those lakes, the most distinguished are: the Big, the Pine tree lake, the Black lake and the Lake of Flowers.

In the southern part of the Park you can find the "Filed of Mares", whose diverse vegetation with multicolor flowers and century-old coniferous trees creates a relaxing environment.

The Park's flora is characterized by two tiers: beech and alpine. Coniferous woods are among the richest in variety in the country and unmatched in the whole Europe.

Lura Park is a potential destination for echo- tourism, winter sports, horse-riding, etc.

The National Park "Pisha e Divjakës" (The Pine-Tree of Divjaka),

This park is located just 5 km from Divjaka and approximately 40 km from the center of the town of Lushnja. Divjaka Park constitutes one of the most important ecosystems in the whole of Albania thanks to the rich fauna sustained by numerous and diverse habitats. It is part of the ensemble of the Lagoon of Karavasta, an area under the protection of the International Convention of Ramsar from the year 1994.

The Park vegetation is mostly coniferous with plants like the wild pine-tree, and less frequently, the cultivated variety. What draws attention is its multilayered character, starting with herbaceous plants to move up to high pine-trees with umbrella-like tops. Besides the coniferous, one encounters also the deciduous varieties like ash, elm-tree, black hornbeam, etc.

Thee diverse habitats of this Park are used as winter destinations, for nesting, or migration by many kinds of birds. Observations made so far have recorded 229 kinds.

The most characteristic inhabitant is the curly pelican (pelicanus crispus), whose colony represents nearly 6.4% of its population worldwide. Karavasta is the westernmost nesting location of this bird in Europe. Tern, a species under grave danger of extinction, lives in the park too.

In the Park, the visitors can engage in echo-tourism, blue tourism, hunting, seafowl observation, fishing, etc.

The National Park "Bredhi i Drenovës" (Fir of Drenova)

This national park is situated 10 km away from the city of Korça and lies against the Mountain of Morava. It is one of the closest national parks to residential areas and mostly frequented by the inhabitants of Korça and the surrounding villages.

The Park is often frequented by the visitors due to its water springs that remain active throughout the year. The most distinguished ones are the spring of Shën Gjergji (Saint George), the spring of the Old Woman, the spring of Pilica, the springs of Izvor and the spring of the Bear.

The Park is dominated by woods of fir. The black pine and mountain maple also grow there. The fauna of the Park is also very rich and well developed. The populations of the big mammals, such as the bear and wolf are significant from a regional point of view. There one

In this Park you can also find some interesting relief formations carved by the wind, like "Guri i Capit" (the Stone of Cap), which has the shape resembling a sitting camel.

The Park has undisputable potentials for the promotion of ecotourism, winter sports, mountain climbing, excursions, etc.

. . .

The National Park of "Lugina e Valbonës" (the Valley of Valbona)

The Valley of Valbona is situated in 25 – 30 km away from the town of Bajram Curri and lies in between high rugged mountain tops, amidst a fantastic blend of colors in every season, giving it an air of mystery and surprises. It has wonderful and unpolluted scenery.

Its configuration, morphology, water resources, woods, pastures, diversity of flowers, the characteristic houses, the generosity and hospitality of the inhabitants create excellent conditions for the development of tourism.

This Park has enormous significance from a scientific, touristic, and recreational viewpoint. It has an area of 8,000 ha is considered to be miracle of the Albanian Alps. Moreover, its biodiversity is significant both nationally and internationally. The high rocky mountains, sides covered by woods, the brooks and the Valbona River, create the impression of a giant crater of stunning natural beauty. The River is the biggest of the Alps, and it flows into the Drino River. The waters flow from the slopes of the Mountain of Jezerca (2,693.5 meters) which is the highest point of the Park and the Albanian Alps. Its waters are clean, clear and transparent up to one meter deep and is rich in silver trout. It runs through a diverse terrain, suitable for sightseeing, fishing, relaxation, recreation, mountain climbing and winter sports.

Additionally, there are many caverns and caves inside the Park.

The most well-known cave is the Cave of Dragobia, which

served as shelter for Bajram Curri (Albanian national hero and leader). Besides its unique forests that match the beautiful landscape of the surrounding area, other vegetation in the Park includes the beech, mountain pine-wood, chestnut, walnut, apple, etc. Whereas the most notable mammals are the brown bear, wolf, wild cat, wild goats, etc.

National Park of "Qafë Shtamë" (Shtama Pass),

You will find this national park located 25 km to the northeast of the town of Kruja. The whole scenery of the Park has a round shape and is very charming.

The most striking feature of this Park is the fountain of "Queen Mother", which has very clear and cold waters. This characteristic, as well as the natural landscape make this Park a a very frequented location. You can find a holiday resort on the northern border of the Park.

The lakes lying close to it, in the northern part, offer good prospects for tourism.

The black pine, oak, juniper, and strawberries make up the flora of the Park.

Among the animals living in it are the wolf, fox, wild boar, mountain partridge, etc. The Park has a lot of potential for the promotion of ecotourism, health tourism (for the illnesses affecting the respiratory tract), mountain climbing, etc.

National Park "Bredhi i Hotovës" (the Fir of Hotova)

If you visit the city of Permet, which is also known as the city of roses and cleanest and greenest city in Albania, only 35 km to its northeast, near the region of Frashër, you will find the the Fir of Hotova. This Park has a very specific shape; it looks like a giant green tiara of visible contrasts, making it very attractive to the eyes of the visitor

Also, by its name it is understandable that the main characteristic featuring this Park is the fir of Hotova, which is regarded as one of the most important Mediterranean relic plants of the country. The black hornbeam, red and black juniper, raspberry, etc. also grow in it. The fauna is quite diverse with animals such as the brown bear, wolf, fox, marten, gazelle, wild bear, wild hare, etc.

Thanks to the wonderful and scenic landscape, the health climate, clean air as well vicinity to residential areas, the Park offers opportunities for tourism, ecotourism, camping, excursions, as well as recreation and sports in every season of the year.

The National Park of "Prespa"

The National Park Prespa is located where the national borders of Albania, Greece and Macedonia meet. It encompasses the lakes of Prespa Major and Prespa Minor, as well as their reservoir basin.

Prespa is distinguished by its rich vegetation consisting of nearly 1,500 kinds, 71 of which trees and undergrowth. Its significance is augmented by its fauna with 6 species of mammals, 15 reptilians and 11 fish.

The area of the Park is also one of the richest historically with the eremite byzantine churches, as well as those post-byzantine such as:

- The cave of Tren in the Lake of Prespa Minor (the Greek

part) where exploration has uncovered signs of a settlement belonging to the early Bronze period;

• The castle of Trajan, one of the major prehistoric settlements in the area; the protective wall in Zvezde, built in the 8th century B.C.;

• The church of Saint Mary in the island of Maligrad, erected in the 14th century.

This region is considered of great potential for tourism, currently unexploited, considering its geographical position as a nodal link between the three neighboring states. The area offers many opportunities for the promotion of tourism, ecotourism, recreation, fishing, gathering and selling of medicinal plants, family tourism, observation of seafowl, blue tourism, water sports, etc. By an agreement signed at the prime ministerial level, the Lake of Prespa Major (the Macedonian part) and that of Prespa Minor (the Greek part) are included in the Balkan Park of Prespa.

Now that you have an idea of the natural beauties and the national park of Albania, let's talk about the things you can do to enjoy this blessed Albanian nature.

Spend a day in the Grand Park in the artificial lake of Tirana

If you are in Tirana and you want to take a rest from the busy city for a while, a visit to Tirana Lake is a must. It is the biggest green area reachable by foot and most of the time the locals come here in the early mornings or evenings, particularly during the weekend.

You can walk or jog, take a coffee or walk and chat with a friend and enjoy the beautiful nature. You can also rent a bike or buggy and ride alongside the lake. In this Park there is an amphitheater, and if you visit Tirana during the summer you might come across some really entertaining cultural events are held. Also, there is a church in the middle of the park.

You can also sit and enjoy the traditional Albanian and Mediterranean food in one of the restaurants along the lake.

Visit the DAJTI Adventure Park

Dajti Adventure Park is really popular among the locals as well as tourists. If you travel with kids, this is the perfect place to spend a day doing outdoor activities. Kids are the ones who love and enjoy Adventure Parks the most. You can reach the park by a car, or by Cable Car. With Cable Car you will enjoy the amazing view above villages and mountains. The entrance fee to Dajti Adventure Park is 10 euros for adults and 8 euros for kids (and price of the Cable Car ride is included in the entrance fee).

Once you arrive you can see why people love this place. This Adventure Park is one more reason to visit Dajti Mountain, from which the view is just remarkable.

This park is for all ages, from children to adults. You will be given the proper uniforms in order to be able to start the climbing journey. For children up to 7 years old there are easy games and trails. The other games were for children above 8 years old and for adults. Neither climbing techniques nor special/specific physical fitness experience are necessary. The difficulty level starts at a low level (yellow trail) and progresses to a very challenging level or “red trail”.

It is a place to have fun, test your courage, and overcome

your own fears and enjoying the beautiful nature in the forest. It is a fantastic experience which you will want to do it again and again!

Try DAJTI Mini Golf

Dajti Mini Golf is the only mini golf field in Tirana. If you are visiting the Dajti Mountain and you love playing golf you can try this new mini golf situated amid the mountainous fresh air. The track is structured with 18 holes, suitable for both for adults and children.

Rock Tirana Climbing Center

This is a fantastic mountain gym, where climbers can challenge their physical limits and learn about this adventurous sport. It is the only gym in Tirana of this kind, close to the Qytet Studenti (the Students' town) in Tirana.

This gym was founded by a young group of climbers who teach the young people about this sport. This gym also organize trainings course, practicing climbing in mountain area of Tirana.

Dig into Tirana's communist past

For nearly 50 years, Albania was under the Communist regime. Although the regime collapsed in 1990, many of Tirana's communist sights remain. Some examples of such remains include the murals and statues in the city center, thousands of bunkers, the house where the communist dictator Enver Hoxha lived as well as the Pyramid, built as his mausoleum.

. . .

Be on the lookout for birds of prey

Pack the binoculars and bird watch in the coastal wetlands of Karavasta. Part of the Divjake-Karavasta National Park, the lagoon is the westernmost breeding site of the Dalmatian Pelican. For further bird watching, visit Kune-Vaini, the nature reserve beside the Drini River, home to spotted eagles, spoonbills and herons.

Outdoor Sports

If you're looking for a way to go deep into wilderness there's nothing quicker than a quick river and rafting trips are the only outdoor activity in Albania that includes deep wild canyons and rivers. While kayaking and canoeing are possible almost all over Albania, in rivers, lakes, and at the coast, amazing rafting trips happen only in Osum and Vjosa rivers.

Hiking and Trekking

Alpine peaks, wide green valleys, glowing lakes, wetlands full of wildlife, traditional villages and a gorgeous coast involving the two seas - the Adriatic and the Ionian Sea are the necessary things for developing hiking and trekking tourism. Albania has it all. Undoubtedly, it has abundant alternative choices to offer you for exciting experiences in outdoor sports. If you are not a professional hiker or do not have sufficient experience it is advices that you participate in organized tours for hiking or go with more experienced local mountain guides.

. . .

Hiking in Valbona and Theth

The most famed, and perhaps most striking, hiking path in Albania is the one from Valbona to Theth, through the Bjeshket e Nemuna (Cursed Mountains). It is a not-to-be missed chance to admire one of the most spectacular landscapes of the Balkan Peninsula and to experience the beauty of the Albanian Alps. As mentioned previously, both Valbona and Theth have been declared national parks of Albania and are two of the most beautiful ones of the country.

It is also called Peaks of the Balkans, because it also crosses over into the neighboring countries of Kosovo and Montenegro, follows an old mule track, is almost 20 km long, and can be completed in one day because it takes a total of eight hours with several stops to enjoy the picturesque views.

The Blue Eye of Kaperre

Albania has two Blue Eyes, the one near Saranda in the south and the Blue Eye of Kaperre. The Blue Eye is a natural pool formed by the erosion of the cliff by the river that created several waterfalls and swimming holes. If you are hiking in Theth and you want to visit the gorgeous **Blue Eye of Kaperre**, you need to walk a lot: from Theth you need to pass through Grunas Canyon and Kaperre, then you'll arrive at one of the most incredible places you'll see in your life. The exhausting walk will definitely be worth it!

. . .

Grunas Canyon

Also while in Theth, do not miss one of the most incredible natural places you'll see in Albania,the Grunas Canyon. It can be found on the south side of the Thethi National Park and can be visited only with expert guides that will lead you to admire this gorgeous two-km-long and 60-meter-deep canyon. The path that leads to the canyon is simply gorgeous and offers incredible views over the Thethi River, which with its crystal clear water is the most beautiful river in the country. Also, if you are a fan of canoeing, the river has enough water for canoe sailing year-round. Don't miss the chance to try it!

Biking in mountains

Instead of hiking you can also try cycling in the mountains, which is exciting and provides you invincible views. You can cycle through the Gramoz Mountains from Korça to Përmet. The level is moderate and the end result is priceless. Take your time and enjoy the dramatic landscape of sweeping valleys, rivers and snowy peaks. To refuel, sample the local food in restaurants along the way.

Rafting and Kayaking

With an impressive network of inland waterways, Albania has an abundance of rafting opportunities Bountiful rivers and amazing natural landscapes grant the experience of rafting and/or kayaking in Albania a rush of adrenaline, alongside other pleasant emotions. As a result, these water sports are attracting increasingly more attention, especially in the two destinations which offer different rafting and kayaking packages: the Osumi Canyons and the Vjosa River. For beginners, the Vjosë River offers a gentle introduction whilst white-water rafting through the spectacular Osum River canyons offers more in the way of adrenaline.

Kayaking and Rafting on Osumi River

Osum River in southern Albania near Berat is a great place to do adventurous activities, including kayaking and rafting. Osumi Canyon is the largest in Albanian and it is located in Corovoda - Hambull section of Osumi Valley. It is 13 km long and width varies from 4-35 meters and over 80 meters high. Interesting rock formations and waterfalls are found in some sections of the Canyon. The waterscape of this area appeals to the fans of water sports such as rafting and river hiking in Osumi River and kayaking in Gradeci Canyon. From April to mid-June, the canyon welcomes rafting enthusiasts of these sports from all over Albania, neighboring countries as well as Europe.

The level of difficulty of these outdoor sports depends on the seasonal water level and flow. On average, the river in the canyon is maintained between the grade II / III and does not present dangers out of your line of site. Summer is the best season for river hiking and walking around the shore, as well as you might find and find excellent place to swim in short stretches where there is more water.

It takes about three hours for a completing a rafting or kayaking trip. While rafting depends on the level of river water, kayaking is possible throughout the year. Following June, it is the main activity in the canyon.

There are several guided tours and groups based in Berat and

Corovoda that organize rafting trips in Osumi River. The package often includes accommodation and food. The canyon is clean and there's no pollution until Corovoda city. Some of the agencies that organize such tours are Albania Rafting Group, Off Limits Albania, Outdoor Albania, etc.

Rafting in the Vjosa River

Take a rafting trip in the Vjosa River, which flows at the foothills of the mighty Nemerçka, the highest mountain of Southern Albania. Vjosa, is also known as the last wild river of Europe because nothing stops its flow for more than 270km. In some sections, the river runs through narrow canyons and gorges and in others the river bed reaches a width of two km.

This rafting track is classified as Wild Water II – III (flat running water with small waves). Difficulty level is moderate. As such, it does not present particular hazards for navigation. Normally, you should know how to swim before trying such sports. Although life jackets keep you above water, swimming or floating capacities are an added security in case of falls.

Besides the adrenaline rush, rafting trips to Vjosa River include exploration of nature and local elements such as traditions and cuisine. You might also want to visit Benja thermal baths, Langarica Canyons and the historic center of Benja.

South Outdoor Festival – SOF (Vuno)

South Outdoor Festival is held on the 27th to the 29th of April in Vuno and invites around 3000 thousand participants to join; not only from Albania, but also from neighboring countries and Europe as well. Is the first of its kind in Albania, and gathers the most adventurous sports in a lasting 3-day event that takes place in the South Coastal Region. The festival is a 3-day celebration of nature and adventure situated in the scenic Albanian Southern Coastal region.

This festival is the first of its kind in Albania encapsulating many activities at once, starting from ground activities: hiking, climbing, jeep safari, canoeing, yoga; water activities: stand up paddle, diving, kayak, as well as paragliding. Jala Bay is the main hosting setting for aquatic sports, while across the area many activities ran simultaneously.

SOF is centered on experiencing the uniqueness of the South of Albania, and it invites participants from all over the country and Europe to join in, compete, and have fun.

At the South Outdoor Festival one can: discover the South and its Regions, encounter cultural treasures, appreciate the strong tradition and visit the charming villages of the Southern Coast. In addition to the competitive events and sports activities, the Festival offers a variety of fun activities, starting from games for kids, workshops, parties, live music, open air cinema, to the golden opportunity of indulging in the most delicious specialties of the South Cuisine.

Apart from participating in the sports activities, it is the perfect timing for exploring the Southern Coast, by visiting the beautiful villages of Himara, exploring the local Mediterranean cuisine, experiencing the culture as well as listening to the traditional Albanian music.

ART & CULTURE

ALBANIA HAS A ROUGH PAST, WITH MANY INFLUENCES incorporated into art and culture from the invading countries throughout the history. A part of Illyria in ancient times and later of the Roman Empire, Albania was ruled by the Byzantine Empire for several centuries. Also Albania has remained under the Ottoman ruling for more than four centuries until it proclaimed its independence in November 1912. All of them have left traces into the art and culture of Albania.

Albania has two distinct cultural groups: the *Gegs* in the north and the *Tosks* in the south. These two cultural groups are geographically separated by the River Shkumbin. They have different dialects and also their cultural differences are considerable. With no common written language until 1972, Albanian's have passed their cultural heritage through epic rural songs, both nationalistic and lyrical in style and folklore.

Most of the art during communist rule was socialist realism. This style continued after communism as Albanian artists wanted to inspire national pride in their countrymen. Today, Albanian artists continue to maintain a proud connection to their roots with contemporary music and arts. During the communist ruling the religious institutions such as churches and mosques which presented the Albanian architecture and art work were destroyed. Instead, the soviet symbolism and uniform high-rise blocks replaced much of Albania's earlier architecture. However, you can still find sites that honor the traditional Albanian architecture and art, particularly the UNESCO-designated World Heritage Sites the cities of Berat, Gijirokastra and Butrint.

Berat boasts a thirteenth century castle, several Byzantine churches and a series of mosques dating from the Ottoman era. Much of the architecture of Gjirokastra also exhibits an Ottoman influence. At Butrint, you can view ruins from each period of the town's development, including Greek, Roman, Byzantine and Venetian eras.

The Best Museums in Albania

Even though small in size, Albania has sufficient things to offer to its visitors. You might think of Albania as a place to only spend the summer vacations in one of the stunning beaches of the Albanian Riviera or the lively nightlife in these cities, particularly in Tirana. Nevertheless, in this small country you will find so much more than that. Albania has so much to offer in terms of history and art; so, also don't miss the chance to visit its interesting and gorgeous museums to learn more about the ancient history of this Balkan country.

BunkArt - Tirana

Tirana is one of the most the vibrant capitals of the Balkan area with plenty of things to do and see. If you are art and history admirer there are sufficient museums and art galleries that are worth a visit. Especially, if you are interested to learn something about the modern history of Albania: take an interesting journey through the recent history of the country, from the Italian occupation to the communism. So, once in Tirana, don't miss BunkArt, a striking museum built inside a huge underground bunker that was constructed during the communist-era on the outskirts of Tirana. Difficult to get there by foot, we recommend you take a taxi or bus from the city center at the clock tower, or main road bus stop to catch a bus to Linze. Also, keep in mind to wear some warm clothes, as the museum is underground and it can be cool there.

This bunker was built for the communist dictator Enver Hoxha, to accommodate him in case of a war or nuclear attack. However, Hoxha wasn't able to see the final version of the bunker as he died a few years before the bunker was completed. It has been discovered late and nowadays, it has been converted into one of the coolest history museums and contemporary art galleries.

BunkArt 2 – Tirana

BunkArt 2 is the newest museum opened in the very centre of Tirana, just a few steps from the splendid and recently renewed Scanderbeg Square, behind the Public Order Ministry.

BunkArt2 is another museum you should not miss while in Tirana and Albania. It is smaller than the BunkArt and easily reachable by foot. The 1,000-square-meter (1,077-square-foot) bunker with reinforced concrete walls up to 2.4 meters (8-feet) thick was built between 1981 and 1986 to shelter elite police and interior ministry staff in the event of a nuclear attack.

This museum is dedicated to the victims of the communist regime and brings attention to the activities of the Ministry of Internal Affairs during communism.It shows the visitors how Communist-era police persecuted the regime's opponents. At the entrance, a voice reads the names of those who were convicted and persecuted by the regime. The museum exposes photographs and equipment that illustrate the political persecution of some 100,000 Albanians from 1945 until 1991.

BunkArt 1 and BunkArt 2 were part of hundreds bunkers built over the country as fortifications for Enver Hoxha dictatorial regime, since he has fear of imaginary invasion by the "imperialist United States and social-imperialist Soviet Union. At one time there were rumoured to be as many as 700,000, but the government says 175,000 were built.

House of Leaves

House of Leaves is also one of the latest museums to open in Albania, and probably the most fascinating. This museum, located right in the heart of the city, in front of Tirana's Orthodox Cathedral and close to the National Bank of Albania, is one of the must – sees while in Tirana.

It is considered to be the equivalent of the Stasi headquarters of the former East Germany. The leaves have a double meaning: things hidden in woods, but also the leave of books and files, on people. Those curious to see what was hidden in the HQ of the notorious National Intelligence Service, also known as the House of Spies, will leave speechless.

The original house was built in 1931 with the primary function of a medical clinic. During World War II, under German occupation, it was used by the Gestapo. Immediately after the end of the war it was regained by the Albanian government and utilized as a security office for investigations. In January 2015, the idea to transform the house into a museum was introduced to the public. The museum was open for the public on 23 May 2017.

The Museum of Medieval Art, Korça

This museum is a must-see attraction for history and art lovers thanks to its large collection of more than 7,000 items of immeasurable cultural significance, such as stones, jewelry, fine metals, textiles, and papers found in the area. The best part of the collection is represented by the paintings and religious icons remembered by some of the most important Albanian artists of the past like Onufri, the Zografi brothers, David Selenica, and so on.

Marubi National Museum of Photography, Shkodra

Located in the beautiful Pedonalja of Shkodra, the most important town north of Albania, Marubi Museum hosts Albania's best photography collections.

Open in 2016, the museum displays the impressive work of

the Marubi family, starting with Pietro Marubbi, an Italian painter and photographer who escaped from Italy for political reasons in the nineteenth century and emigrated to Shkodra, where he founded the first photo studio in the country. The collection includes the first photograph taken in Albania by Marubi in 1858, town life in Shkodra, street scenes and several public events.

National Museum George Castrioti Skanderbeg

The ancient town of Kruja is known to be the home of the greatest Albanian hero of all time, George Kastrioti Skanderbeg. During the fifteenth century, Skanderbeg made Kruja a bastion of resistance against the advance of the Ottoman Empire. Everything in Kruja is related to the national leader: the big statue located at the entrance of the old town, the souvenirs sold in the lovely ancient market and the gorgeous Skanderbeg Museum. The museum hosts beautiful paintings representing battle scenes, giant statues of Skanderbeg and other warriors, as well as a dramatic battle mural located in the first room.

National History Museum, Tirana

If you are planning to visit Tirana, you can't miss the largest museum in Albania, the National History Museum. You can easily find it because it is located in the central Skanderbeg Square and has a gorgeous colored mosaic that represents the most important phases of Albanian history. The museum displays the history of the country from Paleolithic to communist rule. The highlights here are a gorgeous exhibit of icons by Onufri and the replica of Skanderbeg's massive sword used to fight the Ottomans.

If you are keen to know the turbulent history of the Albanians, this is the place to visit. The National History Museum is the most important museum in Albania and contains a well-documented history of the country.

The museum is divided into eight pavilions: Antiquity, Middle Ages, Renaissance, Independence, Iconography, National Liberation Anti-fascism War, Communist Terror, and Mother Teresa. The Pavilion of Communist Terror hosts images, documents and videos of the persecution suffered by the Albanians during the communist regime.

National Museum Of Education, Korça

Korça is considered by Albanians to be the cultural capital of the country because of its cultural importance. The town is home to the first Albanian language school, which officially opened March 7, 1887, under the Ottoman Empire. The National Museum of Education is located inside the building that hosted the first school of the country, near the Pedonalja, the large pedestrian street that connects to the majestic Cathedral of the Resurrection of Korça. The museum displays books and copies of the first written Albanian alphabet, as well as photos of national heroes who contributed to the opening of the school.

Mezuraj Museum

Opened in 2007, the Mezuraj Museum takes visitors on a journey through Albania's past and present, featuring a vast archaeological collection, but also a modern art gallery with sculptures, drawings, paintings and watercolor creations by some of Albania's most accomplished artists. The museum displays the works of top contemporary Albanian painters such as Artur Muhharemi, Helidon Haliti, Gazmend Ieka, Pano Kondo or sculptor Adnan Bushati. Moreover, its permanent exhibition also includes the paintings of Kole Idromeno, the founder of the Albanian painting school of realism from the late 19th century.

Gjirokastër Museum

Discover the relics of Albania's history and culture through the centuries at. Overlooking an important traveling route along the river, the fortress has taken a prominent position in the city's history since the 12th century. The buildings inside date from different time periods and have various functions, such as churches and storage spaces. Take your time walking around, noting the clock tower, cistern, towers, houses, Gjirokastër Museum, and an open courtyard that hosts an annual folk culture festival.

Venice Art Mask Factory, Shkoder

Venice Art is one of the most interesting factories and shops in Shkoder. It is a privately held, family-owned company with headquarters in Shkoder, Albania, and with main offices in Venice, Italy and Las Vegas, USA. Founded in 1998 by Edmond Angoni and it is one of the leading manufacturers in the world for the baroque hand crafted luxury Venetian masks in papier mache and ceramic.

Venice Art was creates beautiful products using the same traditional Venetian techniques and combining them with new exploration and contemporary decoration.

Each unique piece in the Venice Art collection is hand

crafted by highly skilled, dedicated artisans. Traditional craftsmanship is infused into all of the products and every item in their collection echoes the love and skill of the hands that made it. Using techniques handed down through the generations.

If interested you can go and buy a mask among 1700 and more choices. However, if you are not going to buy any mask this factory and showroom is really interesting and worth visiting. Those masks not only look beautiful, but definitely will give you a taste of Venice in the middle of Shkoder!

Art Galleries

Albania is not only a place of contrasts, troubled history and scenic landscapes, but also a destination that can surprise its visitors with a growing cultural life and a vivacious art scene dominated by young and passionate artists. Discover some of the contemporary art galleries in Albania.

Tirana Ekspres

Tirana Exkpres is perhaps the most notable local NGO active in the cultural field and an alternative option for those who wish to discover another side to the Albanian capital. Started as a voluntary project by a small group of dedicated professionals with the aim of creating high quality events, Tirana Ekpres is one of Tirana's main cultural promoters today, attracting over 6,000 visitors of all ages. The gallery's events vary from art exhibitions featuring contemporary artists from all over Europe to music concerts, film festivals such as Zoom (a shorts and documentary film night) or theater and dance spectacles like 5 Rhythms – The Wave Dance.

Albanian National Gallery of Arts

Having opened more than 50 years ago, the Albanian National Gallery of Art is the most representative cultural venue of its kind in Tirana and an excellent starting point for discovering the capital's art scene. The National Gallery features temporary exhibitions of local and international contemporary artists, but also permanent collections of the most important Albanian artists, starting with the late 19th century and continuing with creations of the academically minded Drawing School, a major Albanian artistic movement from the first half of the 20th century. A major attraction is the collection of social realist paintings that translate into art the idea of the 'New Man' during the communist period, with the 'common worker' as the main recurrent personage.

The National Gallery of Arts is a state institution under the care of the Ministry of Culture. The beginnings of the National Arts Gallery can be traced back to the endeavors of a group of Albanian artists and the Arts Committee of 1946. It has changed location several times. The current venue opened on 29 November 1974, and is situated on the Martyrs of the Nation Boulevard. The gallery currently houses 4626 artworks and more than 600 registered artists in the archives. The Gallery of Arts is the only national institution that exhibits, conserves, studies, restores, publishes, documents and archives the works of art in the country.

. . .

Tirana Art Lab Contemporary Center

The result of a bold and recent initiative, Tirana Art Lab is a one-of-a-kind presence in Albania's cultural life. Founded four years ago, this contemporary art center aims to promote emerging artists from Albania as well as other Central, Eastern and Southern European countries. By organizing events such as residencies, exhibitions, workshops, lectures and talks, the center aims to act as a space for critical and reflexive thought that engages with Albanian reality and, in general, with the current neoliberal world order. In a very short period of time, Tirana Art Lab managed to become a popular fixture on Tirana's art scene, representing artists such as Leone Contini, Haus am Gern, Nico Angiuli and Nikolin Bujari.

Tirana Institute of Contemporary Art (TICA)

The first contemporary art center in Tirana, TICA is one of Albania's main actors in promoting local creatives. The center organizes film festivals, exhibitions and the country's most important art event – the Tirana International Contemporary Art Biennale that brought together artists from all over Europe in an attempt to promote and integrate contemporary art. TICA also supports international artist residency programmes with specific areas of focus, for example storytelling as an artistic practice. The programme attracted young participants from Eastern Europe, such as theater director Enton Kaca, Bosnian multimedia artist Adela Jušić and young Georgian painter Keto Logua.

The Promenade Gallery

Located on the beautiful and less-known Albanian Riviera, in Vlora, the Promenade Gallery is a special art space with a vibrant art collection from various genres and techniques. Owned by a painter and enthusiastic art collector, the gallery aims to 'foster new horizons in art', but also 'to restore Vlora's dimension as one of the natural organic centers of the Mediterranean basin'. The gallery exhibits creations of artists such as Israeli video artist Yael Bartana, Swiss video artist Pipilotti Rist, also represented by Hauser Wirth, as well as creatives like Marco Fantini, Ardian Isufi, Rosa Barba and Albanian painter Alkan Nallbani.

The Art Gallery of Pogradec

Pogradec is a charming Albanian city on the coast of Lake Ohrid, in the eastern-central part of the country. A preferred holiday destination with many natural and cultural attractions, this location has several unmissable art galleries starting with the central city Pogradec Art Gallery. A series of small private contemporary art galleries complete the scene and help culture enthusiasts discover the rich creativity of local-born artists. Not to be missed are the Taso Gallery displaying the works of painter Anastas Konstandini-Taso, the Lako Gallery featuring the creations of Skender Laco and woodcarving studio Icka..

Art Gallery E Rira

The art gallery E.RIRA, is founded in 1997 in Tirana, by artist Edmond Rira a private studio of Rira family. In a very short period, within some years, the studio gained a wide professional experience related to the work of art it exhibits all the time, now including even the works of other talented Albanian artists.

All art lovers will find at our Art Gallery E.RIRA works of contemporary artists, who adopts various techniques and genres of figurative art, such as: sculpture, ceramics, paintings, drawings, sketches and mixed techniques. It's always opened for public.

The entrance is free. You can have a coffee, read a book and enjoy the latest piece of art work.

Gallery Kalo

Gallery Kalo is situated close to Mother Theresa Square just before reaching the entrance of Tirana Big Park. In GALERIA KALO you can appreciate great pieces of artwork by Albanian renowned artists, including works of ambitious young modern artists. Kalo Gallery contributes to knowing Albania through the beauty of still life, real life, landscape, portrait and composition. Each month there is a new exhibition with different art collections of various Albanian and international artists. The gallery is supporting especially young artists, but also works from disabled artists or artists with Down syndrome.

Theaters

Theatre was created to portray and reflect on life. This is true for Albanian theatre. Every new play is a reflection of the mood of Albanians in different periods. We have years of brilliant comedies, and years full of dramas. Each night can be spent in a different theatre, enjoying the wonderful performances of Albanian artists, soaking up the atmosphere and being part of it.

The National Theatre

It is the main theatre in Tirana. It has brought so many emotions and so much pleasure to theatre lovers. The present building dates to 1939. It was initially named the Kosovo Cinema. The theatre was inaugurated on 24th May, 1945, and was named the Professional Theatre of Albania. Later, during the communist regime, it was renamed the People's Theatre, keeping that name until June 1991 when it became the National Theatre, as it is now. The first play performed here was a comedy entitled Topazi, directed by Sokrat Mio.

Since then there have been countless plays performed on its stage. The best Albanian artists have performed among its scenes, greeted with ovations from the audience. The stage became a school for young artists. During the communist regime, not only were Albanian dramas performed here, but also those of foreign classic authors. From the 1990s, a number of comedies have been performed, some of which are still very popular and much loved by the Albanian public, such as Pallati 176 and 8 Persona plus.

Metropoli Theatre or Tirana Theatre

It was founded in 2008. It is part of Cultural Center of Tirana, includes: Theater Metropol, Tirana Folk Ansamble, the City Band, Ten Center, the Agimi Cinema and Lapraka Cinema. The focus of this Center is to offer the city the best artistic experience, inviting into the scene all the artists, who love the theater. Metropoli Theater is dedicated to bring a unique artistic life in stage, including the qualitative plays from Albanians authors and International well known plays as well. It offers also great shows for children, for teens and for adults, focusing on professionalism and education of all generations.

The Theater is open for all new talents. It has two halls with a capacity 220 persons, a library including foreign books.

ArTurbina

Opened in July 2th, 2018, "**ArTurbina**" is a multifunctional art center, a modern art space dedicated to cultural and artistic life of the capital, Tirana.

It is called Turbina, (ArTurbina) because of the origin of this building. It used to be a Hydro Turbine Laboratory during communist regime. After the regime collapsed this building degraded and become a rubbish bin in one of the most beautiful areas of Tirana, close to Big Park and Artificial Lake.

The new theatre has two stages, one with 400 seats and other with 150 seats. The building offer best technology for stage performance and shows. There are also spaces for exhibitions, where young and internationals artists will present their work.

The Puppet Theatre

It was founded in 1950 by a professional group of actors, and has been located in the same building for more than 65 years, an interesting historical and symbolic fact. Prior to World

War II it served as the Albanian Parliament, but in the 1950s it became a lovely place for entertaining children. You can find it next to Skanderbeg Square. During communism, it was the only puppet theatre in Albania. In recent years some others theatres have opened to entertain children, but the Puppet Theatre continues to be the popular choice. It gives about 500 performances a year using string puppets, puppet dolls, masks, mimes and performances by various actors. At the weekend tickets are hard to find.

Tirana Circus

Tirana Circus - was founded in 1952 by a group of well-known Albanian artists: Telat Agolli, Bajram Kurti, Xhuzepina Prendi (Shkurti), Bardhyl Jareci and Abdyl Karakashi. The Big Top is still located next to Boulevard Zogu I, close to the centre of Tirana.

The circus had its most successful years during the communist era, after which it had difficulties when its personnel was reduced. A United Nations Development Programme (UNDP) project financed some of its activities and since 2010 Tirana Circus has increased its activities and performances. The circus has been placed under the administration of the Ministry of Tourism, Culture, Youth and Sports. The circus has been known to include famous Albanian athletes among its stars. It gives weekly performances, on Sundays, and is still popular despite its difficulties.

Experimental Theater "Kujtim Spahivogli"

The National Experimental Theatre Kujtim Spahivogli is a

new theatre in Tirana created in 2014 by a government decision in order to present all types of contemporary arts, replacing the Comedy Theatre and occupying the same building. This theatre will present the full range of innovative works and new concepts and techniques in stage production. It houses the Experimental Theatre for Children, and for Youth, the School of Experimental Theatre, and the Oratory School. The Experimental Theatre is part of the National Theatre. It was named for the People's Artist Kujtim Spahivogli who created and directed the Youth Theatre in the former Arts Institute.

Resort Theater Park Kame

Resort Theater Park Kame was created in 2006 by the well-known Albanian theatre director Mr. Gëzim Kame. Only 20 km from the center of the Albanian capital, Tirana, this resort is located in Ibë village at Erzen riverbank, in magnificent Tirana's highlands nature. During the evenings in summer season Kame Resort brings well-known artists on the stage and good music shows for art-lovers . It is the Only Open Air Theater in Tirana, and some of most popular plays are shown during. After the show, all the invitees can enjoy traditional food, walks around the area, entertain kids etc .The resort offers also accommodation in nice wooden bungalows. Visitors can also practice golf in the wide field in front of the resort.

Opera and Ballet

The National Ensemble of Songs and Dances

It undertakes the recording and analysis, development and dissemination of Albanian's ancient and contemporary folk music and dance, including its range of musical instruments and choreography. Traditional costumes and choruses are the key elements in the National Folk Ensemble. Equal to the unique sounds, the costumes are among the greatest national assets, not only from their originality, but also from the variety of colours, patterns and decorations. The Ensemble Choir has a repertoire that few other ensembles today possess. In 2012, the Albanian musician Shkelzen Doli and his ensemble performed Albanian folk music at the Vienna New Year concert, to great success.

The National Symphony Orchestra, with its 60 instrumentalists, has performed in Tirana and on stages around the world, with conductors, instrumentalists, singers and dancers from Albania and from abroad. Famous international composers and conductors have highly appreciated the professionalism of the orchestra. After the collapse of communism in Albania all of its institutions suffered from a lack of funding, forcing many to emigrate. But some of its artists have excelled on the world scene, becoming ambassadors of Albanian art and the spirit of the country.

National theatre of opera and ballet

It is the largest theatre in the country, and its two entities are resident in a fairly new building built in 1953. This theatre has helped develop art in the capital city, as prior to 1953 the singers and dancers had no residence. Located in Skanderbeg Square, the Opera and Ballet belongs to a network of opera and ballet houses in central and Eastern Europe. The first opera to be performed here was Traviata, on 9 December 1956 and directed by Mustafa Krantja with the eponymous heroine sung by Marija Kraja.

Note: The Theatre of Opera and Ballet is relocated in another building and will continue its activity for 3 years in Kinostudio (neighborhood).

9 789518 771718

Printed by Libri Plureos GmbH in Hamburg,
Germany